Managing Projects
Large and Small

The Harvard Business Essentials Series

The Harvard Business Essentials series is designed to provide comprehensive advice, personal coaching, background information, and guidance on the most relevant topics in business. Drawing on rich content from Harvard Business School Publishing and other sources, these concise guides are carefully crafted to provide a highly practical resource for readers with all levels of experience. To assure quality and accuracy, each volume is closely reviewed by a specialized content adviser from a world-class business school. Whether you are a new manager interested in expanding your skills or an experienced executive looking for a personal resource, these solution-oriented books offer reliable answers at your fingertips.

Other books in the series:

Finance for Managers
Hiring and Keeping the Best People
Managing Change and Transition
Negotiation
Business Communication
Creating Teams with an Edge
Manager's Toolkit
Managing Creativity and Innovation

Managing Projects Large and Small

The Fundamental Skills for Delivering on Budget and on Time

Harvard Business School Press | *Boston, Massachusetts*

Library of Congress Cataloging-in-Publication Data
Harvard business essentials : managing projects large and small.
    p. cm. — (The Harvard business essentials series)
Includes bibliographical references and index.
ISBN 1-59139-321-3
1. Project management. I. Title: Managing projects large and small.
II. Harvard Business School. III. Series.
HD69.P75H3745 2004
658.4'04 — dc22
2003026981

The paper used in this publication meets the requirements of the American
National Standard for Permanence of Paper for Publications and
Documents in Libraries and Archives Z39.48-1992.

Contents

Managing Projects
Large and Small

Introduction

Project management is an important tool of modern management, particularly for big jobs, unique jobs, and jobs that require many skills. We define *project management* as the allocation, tracking, and utilization of resources to achieve a particular objective within a specified period of time. This form of management focuses on the characteristic activities of a *project*, namely, a set of activities that (1) aims to produce a unique deliverable (for example, a new commercial airframe) and (2) is time-bound within clear beginning and ending points. The act of designing a new passenger car, for example, fits this definition of a project. Its deliverable may be defined as a unique set of market-tested vehicle specifications that can be manufactured. Once those specifications are complete and the new vehicle goes into production, the project ends; responsibility for the car's production, marketing, sales, and service is handed over to established departments or business units.

Rapid change and the pressures of intense competition have caused more and more organizational work to become project work. Change in technology and in customer demand has made work less routine and less repeatable—that is, it's become more unique and less approachable by business departments that are geared to day-to-day routines. At the same time, competitive pressures have forced enterprises to do their work more quickly.

Naturally, getting a project to deliver on time and on budget requires good management. And the bigger the project, the more challenging good management becomes. A project manager is expected to transform what begins as a vague concept in the collective mind of top management into a measurable and accountable system that directs a broad array of knowledge, skills, and resources to an important organizational goal. In a word, project management—and the people who direct it—helps organizations to get big, important jobs done. The benefits of effective project management can be immense. These are just a few:

- Getting things done on time and on budget. Doing so adds predictability to the business.

- Minimizing development time. By finding ways to deliver on objectives within reasonable planning horizons, project management reduces risk.

- Effective use of resources. Sound project management doesn't waste money or the time of valuable employees.

Given these benefits, it's not surprising that the techniques of project management are being applied to major construction jobs, the development of military and commercial aircraft, e-commerce site construction, motion pictures, and many other complex jobs—even political campaigns.

Origins

The goal setting, organizing, planning, and managing at the heart of project management are nothing new and were surely practiced in one form or another in the past. The grand constructions of the ancient world—Egypt's pyramids, Rome's monumental buildings and road and water systems—have most of the hallmarks of modern-day projects. None would have been completed without substantial engineering, financing, human labor, and, yes, management. The late nineteenth century was likewise characterized by projects of amazing complexity and scope: the first skyscrapers, continent-spanning railroads, and the construction of massive steam-powered ships.

By the early twentieth century, innovators in the field of civil engineering were beginning to think more systematically about the work they faced. They began listening to advocates of scientific management, and, by the 1930s, some of the techniques used by contemporary professional project managers came into use. Hoover Dam, built between 1931 and 1935, made extensive use of a graphic planning tool developed by Henry Laurence Gantt—the now familiar Gantt chart. During World War II, the Manhattan Project developed the first nuclear weapon. In the late 1950s, DuPont, aided by the computing technology of Remington Rand Univac, applied the now familiar critical path methodology to the job of coordinating complex plant operation and maintenance. At roughly the same time, the consulting firm of Booz • Allen & Hamilton was working with the U.S. Navy to create Program Evaluation and Review Technique (PERT), whose charts and schedules were integral to the development of the enormously complex Polaris nuclear submarine program.

Since those formative years, project management techniques have diffused from their origins in civil engineering, construction, and the defense industry to many other fields. Perhaps your company has created a project around the installation of "enterprise resource planning" software, the development of its e-commerce site, or some other major undertaking. Some companies, in fact, organize themselves around sets of major projects. Instead of organizing their activities around conventional departments (finance, marketing, etc.), these companies subsume those functions within the handful of key projects that define their businesses. Microsoft is one such company. Although it has traditional departments, Microsoft's project organizations (Office, Windows, and so forth) are much more important to the success of the company and define how it operates.

Growing Professionalism

Given the diffusion of project management techniques among companies in a wide range of industries, it is not surprising that organizations are getting better and better at planning and structuring work. Those techniques have also become the focus of training courses, consulting services, and certification programs.

The growing professionalism of project management can be seen in the growth of its organizations. The Netherlands-based International Project Management Association (www.ipma.ch), for example, has chapters located throughout Western Europe, Russia, and in a number of developing countries. It provides training, holds conferences on project management issues and sponsors technical publications. Meanwhile, the Project Management Institute (www.pmi.org), headquartered in the United States near Philadelphia, has more than 100,000 members in 125 countries around the world. The institute sponsors research and publications and maintains a rigorous, examination-based certification program to advance the project management profession. It supports research aimed at expanding the body of knowledge on project management and provides training through periodic seminars and online courses.

The only dark side to increased professionalism and consensus on how projects should be managed is this: People may have learned too well how to plan their work and to work their plans. The problem is that it is very hard to spell out everything in advance. The future unfolds in surprising ways as project teams move forward. That is particularly true in fast-moving industries. Every book on this subject will tell you that project managers must be prepared for surprises, and that plans must be sufficiently flexible to accommodate those surprises. Everyone understands this. The result is more attention to risk management, the part of project management that attempts to anticipate and plan for what can go wrong. What if our prototype fails? What if customer requirements change before we finish the project? Contingency plans are developed to deal with these risks.

Unfortunately, people cannot anticipate all the things that can go wrong, nor can they think of all the opportunities they will encounter along their journey—opportunities that should encourage the team to consider scrapping its old plan in favor of something new. Worse, once plans and schedules are agreed upon and set down in planning documents, they become untouchable. Those who deviate from these plans or fail to deliver on time and on budget risk losing favor with management. In making plans and schedules untouchable, executives sometimes unwittingly foster dysfunctional behavior in which problems are swept under the rug and individuals who sound the alarm are ignored or cast out. This is not unusual. Everyone with substantial experience in the field can point to one or another project that, on the surface, appeared to be on track, only to fail in the final stretch because people were afraid to say anything about known problems. Those problems invariably come home to roost in the final weeks or months, when it's too late to do anything about them. This behavioral problem will be addressed at two points in this book, where balancing planning and adaptation are most relevant. Project managers must learn to fulfill expectations formed at the beginning of a project and learn to make midcourse adjustments.

What's Ahead

Like other books in the Harvard Business Essentials series, this one is not designed to make you an expert, nor will it lead you through lengthy academic research. Instead, it provides the action-oriented advice you need to quickly become more effective. It addresses the two essential aspects of the subject: (1) the techniques of project management (design, planning, execution, and so forth) and (2) the many team-specific issues that are absolutely necessary for success. The team component of project management is of critical importance, yet is overlooked in many books.

Chapter 1 will introduce you to the big picture, briefly describing the four processes involved in project work: defining and organizing the project, planning, managing project execution, and closing down the project once the job is done. Subsequent chapters describe those processes in much greater detail.

Chapter 2 reveals the cast of characters typically involved in project work: the sponsor, project manager, team leaders, and team members. Each player has roles and responsibilities, and they are spelled out here.

The next chapter, chapter 3, takes a leaf from the operating manual for team-based work. Like every team, a project needs a charter that states what it will do, the time frame over which it will operate, the resources at its disposal, and the deliverables expected by the sponsor and other key stakeholders. In the absence of a signed charter, the project team cannot be certain of its objectives or the expectation of stakeholders. Worse, at the end of the road, the sponsor might say, "That's not what I meant!" It happens.

Once it has its charter, a project is ready to roll. But not so fast. Internal operating issues must be addressed and agreed to. These include how decisions will be made, a method of keeping track of unresolved questions, a plan for communicating with project members and stakeholders, and so forth. Such internal issues are covered in chapter 4.

Chapter 5 introduces one of the foundational techniques of project management: work breakdown structure (WBS). You cannot plan a project if you don't have a firm grasp on this technique. WBS decomposes the project into a set of manageable, bite-sized tasks, with an estimate of the time and money needed to complete each.

If you take care to think of everything that must be done to meet your objective, you will be ready for the next chapter, on scheduling the work. Scheduling begins with understanding the dependencies that exist between the tasks defined through WBS. Dependencies matter. For example, when you get ready for work in the morning, it's best to take a shower *before* getting dressed. Wouldn't you agree? And when you do get dressed, it's wise to put on your socks before you put on your shoes. Handling those tasks in the wrong order would create quite a mess. It's the same with project tasks; some must wait until others are completed—or partially completed. Others can be done in parallel. You'll learn about task dependencies in chapter 6, and you'll also read about how you can use that knowledge to schedule tasks using project tools such as Gantt and PERT charts. The important issue of the critical path is also explained.

Work breakdown structure and scheduling often uncover discrepancies between what is possible and what is specified in the charter and in the stakeholders' expectations. You may, for example, have a boss who insists on project completion within four months with a budget of $200,000. If satisfactory completion under the existing terms is impossible, trade-offs and adjustments—the subject of chapter 7—will have to be made.

Chapter 8 is about managing risk. Project planning involves the future, which is bound to contain surprises and setbacks. What are the major risks facing your project? Will the scientific staff fail to produce a working prototype on schedule? What would happen if a key supplier went out of business or delivered substandard materials? This chapter will show you how to identify your risks, take actions to avoid or minimize their impact, and develop contingency plans. The subject of risk is continued in chapter 9, but here the focus is on the risks that you cannot reasonably identify or anticipate. It proposes an adaptive project management approach as a solution. That approach emphasizes small incremental steps followed by evaluation and adjustment, fast cycles, early value delivery, and rapid learning by project team members.

Chapter 10 is about two preparatory details that must be tended to: the all-important project launch and team-based work. The launch section explains the why and how of project launch meetings. This meeting must signal the beginning of an important endeavor—one that is aligned with the organization's highest goals and from which all participants will benefit. It should also provide clear evidence that top management supports the project and its people. The next section of chapter 10 is a primer on the basics of team-based work. It explains how the project leadership must establish norms of behavior, such as meeting attendance, how to give and receive feedback, the importance of confidentiality, and so forth. Unless people understand how to work as a team, success is unlikely.

Chapter 11 tells project managers and team leaders how they can maintain control and keep people's work on track. When resources are finite and deadlines are fixed, they cannot allow individuals and work teams to operate willy-nilly and without coordination. Everyone must work toward the same goals. Four means of maintaining project control are offered in this chapter: budgets that pace spending, turning time-wasting conflict to collaboration, communication, and clearing away problems.

Chapter 12 addresses the fourth and final phase of project management: the closedown. Closedown is almost as important as the project launch. It is the point at which the team delivers its results to the sponsor and stakeholders, thanks people for their contributions, celebrates, documents its work, and then attempts to learn from its experience. Of these steps, learning may be the most important. People must answer the question, If we could start over again tomorrow, what would we change? They will take that answer—and it lessons—to their next projects. And make no mistake, there will be future projects.

The back matter of this book contains four items you may find useful. The first is a set of project management worksheets and checklists. Free interactive versions of them and other tools highlighted in the Harvard Business Essentials series can be downloaded from the official series Web site, www.elearning.hbsp.org/businesstools. Check it out. Chances are that you'll find tools that you can use.

The second item is "A Guide to Effective Meetings." Projects generally have lots of meetings. Most conscientious people dislike meetings, and rightly so, since many meetings are time wasters. But meetings are essential, and effectively run meetings get things done. They aren't time wasters. This short guide will help you prepare for meetings, run them effectively, and follow up for better results.

The third item is a glossary of terms. Every discipline has its special vocabulary, and project management is no exception. When you see a word italicized in the text, that's your cue that the word is defined in the glossary.

Finally, "For Further Reading" identifies books and articles that can tell you more about topics covered in this book. If you want to dig deeper into any aspects of project management, these supplemental sources are readily available.

The content of this book draws heavily on a number of books, articles, and online publications of Harvard Business School Publishing, in particular, the project management and leading teams modules of Harvard ManageMentor®, an online service. All other sources are noted with standard endnote citations.

Project Management As a Process

Four Phases

Key Topics Covered in This Chapter

- *An overview of the four phases of project management*

- *Uncovering the core issues of your project*

- *Identifying your project's stakeholders*

PROJECTS COME in all types and sizes, from building orbiting space stations to installing new information systems. Yet the essential elements of project management are the same. Those elements are typically handled within a four-phase process:

1. Defining and organizing the project

2. Planning the project

3. Managing project execution

4. Closing down the project

This chapter provides an overview of that process.

Figure 1-1 represents the four phases as an integrated model. In one sense, this model is linear: First, we define and organize the project, then we plan the work in detail, and so forth. But the reality of project management is never that tidy. Many aspects of the project cannot be anticipated. Some of those aspects are negative—for example, a key supplier may be hamstrung by a strike, or the project manager may accept an offer to join another company. Others are positive. For example, in the course of developing a new product, a project team member may discover an important new market; in order to exploit that market, the product would require slightly different specifications. Such a discovery represents an important and unanticipated opportunity for the company. But capturing it requires changes in the project's schedule and budget. Thus, the model is not entirely linear, and so there must be feedback loops and

FIGURE 1-1

The Project Management Model

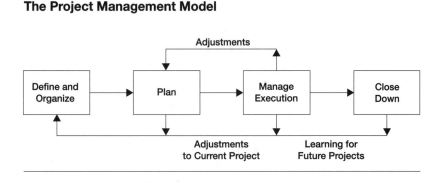

opportunities for readjustment between the four phases. Even the final phase of the model, closing down the project, has a feedback loop that informs the next project start-up. That feedback can help the organization learn from its experience and improve the performance of future projects.

Whether you're creating a backup system for your company's computer network or busily working on the next Martian space probe, you will deal with this four-phase process or something very similar. Each phase is described briefly below, with the details provided in subsequent chapters.

Defining and Organizing the Project

This phase has two purposes:

1. To clearly define the project's objectives as thoroughly as possible

2. To organize the right people and all necessary resources around those objectives

Defining the Objective

In Lewis Carroll's *Through the Looking-Glass*, Alice asks the Cheshire Cat, "Would you tell me, please, which way I ought to go from here?" The cat answers that the right way depends on where she wants to go. "I don't much care where," says Alice, "as long as I get somewhere." The cat replies, "Oh, you're sure to do that, if only you walk long enough."

Obviously, you don't want to be like Alice, wandering endlessly and randomly until, by chance, you arrive at a suitable "somewhere." The best way to get where you are going is to first identify your destination. This commonsense advice seems obvious, but is not always observed in practice. What problem is your project expected to solve? What deliverable does management expect from your team? You may have clear answers to those questions, but not everyone may agree with you. Other project team members, the stakeholders who will use the project's output, and the senior managers who will judge the success or failure of your work may have slightly different expectations. So before you begin to plan the work, make sure that everyone is singing from the same page in the hymn book. Identify the project's objective or objectives in the clearest possible terms. We'll see in chapter 2 how a project charter serves this purpose.

Sometimes it is easy for everyone to agree on objectives. This is especially true when the desired outcome follows clearly from the motivation for the project—for example, when everyone says in unison, "The problem is _____ ." Harvard professors Lynda Applegate, Robert Austin, and Warren McFarlan refer to these situations as "highly structured projects." In describing corporate information-technology projects, they say, "High structure implies that the nature of the task defines its outputs, the possibility of users changing their minds about the desired outputs is practically nonexistent, and significant change management issues are not present."[1] Unfortunately, few project situations are highly structured. Objectives are not always shared. Even the definition of the problem may be unresolved. Consider this example:

> *Senior management has enlisted Sam, manager of the company's IT department, to develop a new database and data-entry system—and he's prepared to start work tomorrow. In fact, he has been waiting all year for the go-ahead to upgrade those parts of the company's IT system. But will his response really address the problem? "I know what*

the problem is," he answers. "Everyone is complaining that they can't get data out the system fast enough. And then they have to sift through many reports to compile the customer information they need to make decisions."

The complaints cited by Sam may be genuine, but they are only symptoms of a problem and don't clearly express user needs. What are those needs? No one knows for certain. People in marketing may cite some data needs, but employees in manufacturing and finance may cite others. Nor is there any indication of *when* the fix is needed, or how much the company is willing to spend to fix the perceived problems.

Here's another example: "Develop a Web site capable of providing fast, accurate, cost-effective product information and fulfillment to our customers." That is how a sponsor described a project's objective. But what exactly does he mean? What is "fast"? How should accuracy be defined? Is one error in 1,000 transactions acceptable, or would one error in 10,000 meet the sponsor's expectation? To what degree must the site be cost effective? Those are all questions that must be answered in consultation with the sponsor. All objectives should be specific and measurable. If they are not, the project team will have no way of knowing whether the sponsor's objectives have been met. One way to achieve clarity on the objective is through a dialogue whose explicit aim is to achieve agreement on (1) the problem or opportunity that motivates the project and (2) what the output of the project team should look like. There should also be a time frame within which objectives will be achieved; the project cannot be open-ended.

The issues described in the examples just given are fairly typical. Objectives must be clarified and agreement on them must be reached before the real work of the project can begin in earnest. Bad things happen when managers fail to do so. In the first example, Sam, the IT manager, runs the risk of wasting time by designing a system that is either too simple or too complicated—or one that doesn't respond to the fundamental concerns of stakeholders. His employer runs the risk of wasting large sums of money and the energy of many key personnel.

Dialogue is one technique for clarifying project objectives. Another, as suggested by Robert Austin, is to develop a prototype of the project's outcome. For example, for a software project, many use a simple working prototype to demonstrate key features and functions. Prototype development takes time and money, but having a tangible, working version of the final output in hand can elicit very useful feedback from stakeholders. Feedback informed by contact with a prototype—such as, "Generally, I like the way this works, but I'd make it easier to use"—will be superior to the sponsor's reaction to a paper document that describes what a hypothetical piece of software might do. It also provides some assurance that you will not get to the end of a long project and hear the sponsor or customer say, "No, this isn't what I had in mind."

What are the real issues at the core of your project? Asking these questions can help you uncover them:

Who Are the Stakeholders?

A stakeholder is anyone with a vested interest in a project's outcome. Likewise, a stakeholder is anyone who will judge a project's success or failure. Project team members, customers, and senior management are all likely stakeholders. To identify the stakeholders in your project, pay attention to the following:

• The functions of individuals who will be affected by your project's activities or outcomes

• The contributors of project resources, including people, space, time, tools, and money

• The users and/or beneficiaries of the project's output

Each is a stakeholder in your project.

- What is the perceived need or purpose for what we are trying to do?

- Why do people see this as a problem that needs to be solved?

- Who has a stake in the outcome?

- How do the various stakeholders' goals differ?

- What criteria will stakeholders use to judge success or failure?

Have those questions answered correctly—and by the stakeholders—and you will increase the likelihood of your project's success.

Organizing the Effort

Once you are satisfied that the project has a clear, unambiguous objective, the next chore is to organize the effort. The moving force behind that step should be either the executive who proposed and authorized the project or the individual appointed as project manager. In either case, someone must create a team that's capable of achieving the project's objective.

At this early stage, the organizer must consider the objective and make a rough-cut determination of which people and what resources will be needed to get the job done. In his book *Strategic Benchmarking*, Gregory Watson provides a glimpse of how this was successfully done in the case of Ford Motor Company's development of the original Taurus automobile model back in the late 1970s. Ford's senior management literally bet their company on the Taurus project, which represented a major break in design from the company's existing vehicles. But it was a bet that paid off hugely for Ford. And project team organization played a major part in that success.

As described by Watson, completion of the project required the involvement of every functional group in the company. The groups participated through a cross-functional team headed by a senior project manager named Lew Veraldi. According to Watson, Veraldi had broad discretion in selecting team members, which he accomplished by mapping all required areas of technical and market expertise needed to produce and launch a new car model. Team membership was represented through two levels: an inner circle of key people numbering less than ten, and a larger set of players numbering over 400. It would take that many to get the job done. Only a fraction of these would dedicate 100 percent of their time to Team Taurus work. Each team member, however, would bring along all the know-how and resources of his or her functional department.[2]

As described here, the mapping exercise identified the people and resources needed to accomplish the mission. Among these was a small core group of influential people who formed, in effect, an executive counsel for the much larger project team. This core group had organizational clout and the authority to allocate resources. While hundreds of others were represented within the project team and its work, this executive council was small enough to make decisions and had the power to make its decisions stick. (You should also note in this example that the leader and core team fit the common definition of heavyweights. Steven Wheelwright and Kim Clark, who developed that term, defined heavyweights as individuals who have both high technical expertise and organizational clout. They bring various strengths and weaknesses to every project effort.)[3]

Your projects are unlikely to be as large and complex as the Taurus project. Nevertheless, organizing the effort should follow a similar approach—namely, identifying and enlisting all the expertise, resources, and people needed to complete the job. The details of assessing the needed skills and resources will be provided in later chapters.

Planning the Project

Planning is the second phase of the project management process. It is a necessary prelude to action. Project planning generally begins with the objective and works backward, in effect asking, "Given our objective of _____ , what set of tasks must we complete?" More accurately, planners must also decide in what order and within what time frame they must complete those tasks. For example, if the objective is to land a cat on the moon within five years and bring her home safely, a rough-cut plan, or feasibility study, might take the form shown in figure 1-2. Here the planner has taken the stated goal and broken it down into a set of key tasks. Just as important, she has created time frames within which each task must be completed for the overall objective to be completed on schedule.

In the project planning phase, each task and subtask is assigned a reasonable time for completion. When they are put into a master schedule (with some done in series and others in parallel), the project manager is able to determine (1) whether some individuals are overloaded while others are not being asked to do enough and (2) the end-to-end time required for the project. If that time is greater than that specified in the charter, adjustments must be made to the scope of the project, to the schedule, and/or to the resources committed by the charter.

The project manager and appropriate team members must then analyze the tasks to determine whether all are necessary and whether some can be redesigned to make them faster and less costly to complete.

FIGURE 1-2

Plan for National Cat in Space Program

Year	1	2	3	4	5
Key tasks					
Design/build cat space vehicle	████	████	████		
Test space vehicle				███	██
Study cat in space physiology	█	█			
Recruit/train cat crew		███	████	████	█
Build launch/recovery systems	████	████	████	███	
Test launch/recovery systems				███	█
Launch/recover cat					█

Managing Project Execution

Once a project is up and running, it must be managed. An unmanaged project will very likely fail. Efforts will be uncoordinated—wasting time and money—or the project's energy will veer off course, producing deliverables that fail to match those stipulated by the sponsor and stakeholders.

Project execution requires all the traditional skills of sound management: keeping people motivated and focused on goals, mediating between the people above and the people below, making decisions, allocating scarce resources to their highest uses, reallocating resources to deal with emerging problems, and so forth. The project manager must also monitor and control adherence to the schedule, budget, and quality standards. And as we will see later, he or she must give particular attention to the kinds of issues that go hand-in-hand with team-based work: interpersonal conflict, collaboration, and communication.

Closing the Project

Closedown is the final phase of project management. By definition, every project has an end point—the time at which objectives are achieved and deliverables are handed over to stakeholders. At that point, the project must fold its tents and its members return to their regular assignments.

Learning is the most important activity of this project phase. Though most participants will be anxious to go back to their traditional duties, they should take time to reflect on their experience. What went well, and what went badly? What could have been improved? Using the benefits of hindsight, how should the project have been planned and executed? The lessons learned through reflection must be recorded and incorporated in future projects. Doing so will put the next project team on a strong footing.

The four phases described above are time tested and highly suitable for most projects. The details of each phase will unfold in the chapters that follow. But as we will learn later, this logical, essentially linear approach is less suitable for projects that face high levels of uncertainty.

Summing Up

- Projects have four basic phases: defining and organizing, planning, managing execution, and closing down.

- Though it would appear that the four phases should be handled one after another, in a linear fashion, the reality of project work is seldom that tidy.

- The tasks involved in the first phase are to clearly define project objectives and to organize the right people and resources around them.

- The moving force behind organizing the effort is either the executive who proposed and authorized the project or the individual appointed as project manager.

- The second project phase, planning, generally begins with the objective and works backward, identifying each of the many tasks that must be completed, estimating the time needed to finish them, and scheduling them in the right order.

- The managing execution phase requires all the traditional chores of effective management as well as careful monitoring and control. Together, they assure adherence to the schedule, budget, and quality standards.

- One of the unique features of a project is that it has a limited life. It ends when objectives are achieved and deliverables are given to stakeholders. The project then terminates, but only after wrapping up loose ends and reflecting on the lessons learned from the experience.

The Cast of Characters

Who's Who in Project Management

Key Topics Covered in This Chapter

- *Understanding the roles of the project sponsor, project manager, project team leader, and team members*

- *Choosing leaders*

- *Selecting team members*

- *The six characteristics of effective teams*

T HE SUCCESS of project work is naturally affected by the people who participate. Yes, a sound organizational structure matters; so does good management. But neither will produce a satisfactory outcome if the right people are not on board—or if those people are not clear about their roles. This chapter identifies the key project players and their roles and responsibilities. Furthermore, it provides advice about the characteristics of effective project managers and project teams and how to select team members.

Project Sponsor

Whether a project is formed by a manager or by a group of staff members, it must have a *sponsor*. The sponsor authorizes the project. He or she should be a manager or executive with a real stake in the outcome and with accountability for the project's performance. The sponsor should also have the authority to define the scope of the work, provide it with necessary resources, and approve or reject the final output. In other words, the sponsor should be a person with real clout—someone who's capable of

- championing the project at the highest level,

- clearing away organizational obstructions,

- providing the resources required for success, and

- communicating effectively with the CEO and key stakeholders.

In their book *Radical Innovation*, Richard Leifer and his colleagues made an important observation about each of the ten cases they studied. That observation is relevant here. They found that in each case a highly placed sponsor, or patron, was instrumental in providing critical services.[1] These sponsors kept their projects alive by providing funding—sometimes through normal channels, and sometimes under the table. They deflected attempts to terminate innovation projects and promoted the value of project goals to higher management. Without the protection and support of these patrons, each of the ten projects would have died or limped along, starving for funds and without a clear conclusion.

The sponsor must protect the project from high-level enemies who see its objective as a threat to their personal turf. This is particularly critical when a project is working to develop products or technologies that, if successful, will cannibalize the sales of current products or render them obsolete. In these instances, powerful executives who represent the current product lines are likely to be hostile to the project's goals and may use their power to withhold funding or disrupt the team's work. Here it is wise to recall Machiavelli's warning in *The Prince* to all who attempt to alter the status quo: "There is nothing more difficult to carry out, or more doubtful of success, nor more dangerous to handle, than to initiate a new order of things. For the reformer has enemies in all those who profit from the old order."

Does your project have an influential sponsor? If it does, is that sponsor acting as a true champion by providing resources and fending off internal enemies? Is the sponsor sufficiently wise to differentiate between unwarranted negativism and criticism that identifies real problems?

If you are a senior executive, think about the people you put forward as sponsors. Are they really committed to their projects' success? Do they act as champions, or are they simply going through the motions? Have you arranged things so that they have a personal stake—such as a bonus—in their teams' success or failure? This last point merits special attention. Sponsors should have "skin in the game." If they have nothing to lose (and perhaps something to gain) from project failure, their usefulness is questionable.

Project Sponsor's To-Do List

- Ensure that the project's progress is communicated to the rest of the organization and to the leadership in particular.

- Ensure that senior management supports the project team's decisions and direction.

- Be alert to any change in company objectives that may affect the project's objectives. Project objectives must be aligned with company objectives.

- Remember that some managers will not want their subordinates splitting their time between project duties and their regular assignments. Work with these managers to smooth over difficulties.

Project Manager

Every project has a single manager. The *project manager* is the individual charged with planning and scheduling project tasks and day-to-day management of project execution. He or she is also the person with the greatest accountability for the endeavor's success. This person receives authority from the sponsor and plays a central role in each phase of the project's life cycle, from design and organization to project closedown and evaluation—and everything in between.

In many respects, the task of the project manager is similar to those of a manager in any other function. Both are charged with obtaining results through people and other resources. And like the traditional manager, the project manager must also

- recruit effective participants;

- provide a framework for the project's activities;

- keep the vision clear;

- coordinate activities;

- negotiate with higher authorities, and with the sponsor in particular;

- mediate conflicts;

- identify needed resources;

- set milestones;

- manage the budget;

- ensure that everyone contributes and benefits;

- keep work on track; and

- assure that project goals are delivered on time and on budget.

Doesn't that sound like the typical manager's role? In big projects it is, in fact, very similar. In these cases, the project manager acts as decision maker, delegator, director, motivator, and scheduler of others' work. He or she is like the traditional boss. On the other hand, the project manager may not have formal authority over the people who do the work. For example, the project manager of a new IT initiative may be the IT manager, but the project members may be drawn from marketing, finance, customer service, and so forth. They are not individuals over whom the project manager has direct authority or the traditional forms of leverage, such as pay raises and promotions, so the project manager must rely on his or her leadership qualities to influence behavior and performance.

Project Team Leader

Many large projects are organized to include a project team leader who reports directly to the project manager, as shown in figure 2-1. In small projects, the project manager wears both hats.

The team leader cannot act like the boss and still obtain the benefits normally associated with team-based work. Instead, the team leader

FIGURE 2-1

Sponsors, Project Managers, Project Team Leaders, and Members

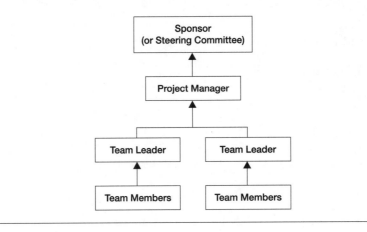

must adopt five important roles: initiator, model, negotiator, listener, and coach. The team leader must also pitch in as a working member.

Leader As Initiator

The team leader must initiate action. Though the effective leader does not tell people what they must do, he or she draws attention to actions that must be taken if team goals are to be met. A good team leader is well positioned to initiate action because he or she usually stands somewhat apart from the day-to-day work of the team, a position from which the connections between that work and the higher objectives of the effort can be more readily observed. While members are deeply enmeshed in tasks and problem solving, the leader is in close contact with the expectations of the sponsor, the project manager, and external stakeholders. Using evidence and rational argument, the leader encourages members to take the steps needed to meet those larger expectations. This is an important function, particularly when those expectations are in conflict with the personal expectations of individual team members.

Leader As Model

Both traditional managers and team leaders can use their own behavior to shape others' behavior and performance. The big difference is that team leaders must rely more heavily on this tactic, since they cannot use promotions, compensations, and threats of dismissal to influence team members.

Model behavior by the team leader is, in fact, a powerful tool. It sets a standard to which others must rise, if only to avoid seeming ineffective or petty. Leaders can model team behavior in many different ways. If team members need to get out of the office and rub shoulders with customers, an effective leader would not instruct them to do so. Instead, he or she would begin a regular practice of traveling to customer locations, creating customer focus groups, and so forth. Team members would be encouraged to participate. In a word, the leader would model a behavior that had a direct impact on team performance.

Leader As Negotiator

"I'd like Bill to join our process-improvement team," the team leader told Bill's manager. The manager frowned; Bill was one of her best performers. "Being part of the team will involve an estimated four hours of work each week," the team leader continued, "that includes meetings and team assignments."

Managers do not particularly welcome requests like that one. The team has goals, but so do the managers who are asked to contribute skilled employees and other resources; complying with a team leader's request can only make their jobs more difficult. Effective team leaders recognize this and use negotiating skills to obtain what they need. The executive sponsor can facilitate the process by making it clear that the project's goals are important to the company and that the cooperation of managers is expected.

The best way to negotiate with resource providers is to frame the situation in a positive way—as mutually beneficial. A mutually beneficial negotiation occurs when both parties recognize opportunities for gain. If you are a project team leader, you will have a better chance of framing your negotiations as good for both parties if you do the following:

- Emphasize the higher-level goals of the organization, and how successful team action will contribute to them. Doing so underscores a point we'll explain later in this book—that project goals must be important and aligned with organizational goals.

- Emphasize how the other party will benefit by helping the project—for example, by indicating how the project's success will contribute to the other party's success.

To be a successful negotiator, the team leader must present himself as trustworthy and reliable and the mutual benefits as realistic.

Leader As Listener

A good leader spends as much time listening as talking. Listening is a sensing activity that gathers signals from the environment—signals about impending trouble, employee discontent, and opportunities for gain. The main benefit of bringing together people with diverse experiences and skills is that different members will have useful knowledge and insights. Team members will be encouraged by a leader who listens to share what they know or perceive. Sensing naturally leads to a response. The leader who listens well generally recommends actions informed by the experience and knowledge of many people.

Leader As Coach

A good team leader finds ways to help team members excel. In most cases, this is accomplished through coaching. *Coaching* is a two-way activity in which the parties share knowledge and experience to maximize a team member's potential and help him or her achieve agreed-upon goals. It is a shared effort in which the person being coached participates actively and willingly. Good team leaders find coaching opportunities in the course of everyday business. Their coaching can help members with many routine activities: to make better presentations, to schedule their work, to deal with intrateam conflict, to obtain external resources, to set up a budget, to develop skills, or even to work effectively in a team environment.

Coaching opportunities are especially prevalent within teams because so many of the skills members eventually need are skills they don't have but must learn as their projects unfold. For example, an engineer recruited because of her technical capabilities may suddenly find that she must prepare and present a businesslike progress report to senior management. She must develop presentation skills quickly—and coaching by the team leader can help.

Leader As Working Member

A project leader must also pitch in and do a share of the work, particularly in areas where he or she has special competence. Ideally, that share will include one or two of the unpleasant or unexciting jobs that no one really wants to do. Pitching in solidifies the perception that the leader is a member of the team, not a traditional boss.

What are the characteristics of a person who can do most, or all, of the things just described? For starters, a team leader should have the leadership skills we are all acquainted with: the ability to set a direction that others will follow, good communication skills, the ability to give and to accept feedback, integrity, and high standards for performance. Beyond these, a project team leader should have a positive attitude toward team-based work—and preferably experience with it. The last person you'd want to fill the job would be someone who insists on acting like a traditional boss.

The team leader should also enjoy credibility among team members. That means having appropriate skills and experience and a reputation for dealing effectively with others. Lack of credibility can lead to ridicule and a highly dysfunctional situation.

Choosing the Leader

The project manager may designate a team leader if the project is of very short duration, if there is an immediate need for a team (as in crisis), or if there is an organizational reason for a certain person to be the team leader (such as giving a competent younger employee an opportunity to learn and practice leadership skills). In other situations, the team may select its own leader—or rotate the leadership post and its responsibilities on a regular basis.

One Leader or Several?

We generally think in terms of a single formal leader. Investing leadership in a single person assures that authority has an undivided voice. How, after all, would a team get things done if it had two bickering leaders? Whose direction would people follow? The experience of teams, however, indicates that investing leadership in a single person is not an absolute necessity as long as there is agreement among leaders on means and ends. The only necessity is that leaders are of one mind as to their goal and its importance.

A project that brings together many people representing two or more technical specialties may, in fact, benefit from multiple leadership, particularly if the leaders report to a single project manager. For example, a team whose goal was to establish a new e-commerce site had a project manager and four area leaders: a technical leader, a user interface leader, a site strategy leader, and a content leader, similar to what is shown in figure 2-1. Each leader reported to the project manager, and each had responsibility for a very unique aspect of the project's work. Within these areas of responsibility, team leaders had authority to make decisions and to allocate resources. Only when their decisions affected other teams, the project plan, the budget, or the schedule were they required to seek approval from the project manager or other high-level authority.

Team Leader's To-Do List

- Regularly communicate progress and problems with the project manager.

- Periodically assess team progress, the outlook of members, and how each member views his or her contribution.

- Make sure that everyone contributes and everyone's voice is heard.

- Do a share of the work.

- Resist the urge to act like a boss.

Project Team Members

The heart of any project, and the true engine of its work, is its membership. Yes, a good sponsor can clear the way and secure resources, and, yes, a good project leader can motivate performance and keep the work focused. But it's the project team members who do most of the work. As a consequence, bringing together the right people with the right skills is extremely important.

Choosing good team members is probably the trickiest part of team design. A team can acquire its members in one or more of the following ways:

- **Assignment**. The sponsor selects the appropriate people and invites them to participate.

- **Voluntary**. The people most invested or most interested in the work step forward as potential members.

- **Nominated**. People who have an interest in the project nominate individuals who have the right skills and in whom they have confidence.

None of these selection methods is inherently better or worse than others. Each is capable of tapping the right members. But each is equally capable of putting the wrong people on a team, particularly when the organization is highly politicized. Consider these examples:

- The sponsor has selected most of the members of a new Web site design team. Hugh, the sponsor's right-hand man, is one of them. Hugh doesn't know a server from a hyperlink and has nothing in particular to contribute to the team effort. His only purpose will be to report back to the sponsor, who distrusts several team members. For the team, Hugh is excess baggage. Other team members will quickly discover his role as informant and react negatively.

- Ann has volunteered to work on a project that's being organized to reengineer the company's order-fulfillment process. Ann isn't particularly interested in the project's objective, but she sees membership as a way to get face time with Katherine, the project manager and a rising manager in the company. Ann is also concerned that her main rival for a promotion is already on the team. "If he's on that team, I had better be on it too," she reasons. It's clear that Ann's commitment is not to the team's objective but to her own self-interest. As a consequence, her value to the project is questionable.

- Harry has volunteered for the same reengineering project. He has a proprietary interest in the current order-fulfillment process and believes that his organizational standing will suffer if the team adopts a radical makeover of that process. His motivation is self-protection, and his commitment is not to the team's objective but to the status quo. He absolutely should *not* be on the team.

- Ralph has nominated Muriel, one of his direct reports, to the Web site design team. "This will be a good learning experience for her," he tells himself. Yes, Muriel's participation might be a very good thing for her career development, but will it be a very good thing for the team? What does she have to contribute?

Do you see examples like those in your organization? If you do, watch out. In each example, an individual was put forward as a project team member for a reason that had nothing to do with helping

the project achieve its stated goals. Such approaches to member selection should be avoided. A case might be made for Muriel's inclu-
sion in the team, however, if she is a fast learner and a hard worker.
But the achievement of project goals must have priority over the development of individual members.

Criteria for Project Team Membership

If having the right people on board is so important, what criteria
should a team leader look for?

SKILL ASSESSMENT. Team selection should ideally be determined by the skills needed to accomplish the work. Skill assessment
is a two-stage process: The first stage looks objectively at a task and
determines exactly what skills are needed to get it done. For example, in examining all the activities that need to be done, the leader
may determine that the team must include members with the following skills: market research, electrical engineering, manufacturing,
and purchasing. Together, they represent all the skills and resources
needed to achieve the project's goal.

Stage two of skill assessment looks at the people in the organization and determines which have the right skills. The right skills
may be categorized as technical, problem-solving, interpersonal, and
organizational.

- **Technical skill** refers to specific expertise—in market research,
  finance, software programming, and so forth. Technical skill is
  usually the product of special training.

- **Problem-solving skill** is an individual's ability to analyze difficult situations or impasses and to craft solutions. Engineers are
  trained as problem solvers. Creative people have habits of mind
  that help them see resolutions that routinely elude others. If
  you're the leader, you need problem solvers on your team; otherwise, people will continually look to you for solutions—and
  that is not a teamwise approach.

- **Interpersonal skill** refers to an ability to work effectively with
  others—a very important trait for team-based work. Don't

overlook it. In practice, interpersonal skill takes the form of interpersonal chemistry. Let's face it, some people naturally get along well with particular people and not so well with others. For example, a straitlaced person with a formal demeanor and no patience for joking and partying will most likely lack the chemistry needed to work well with a group of fun-loving software programmers who come to work on skateboards and end the day with a round of pizza and beer. Businesspeople too often view employees as interchangeable, as long as they have the same skill sets. Don't make that mistake.

- **Organizational skills** include the ability to communicate with other units, knowledge of the company's political landscape, and possession of a network. People with these skills help the team get things done and avoid conflict with operating units and their personnel.

When forming project teams, there is a natural tendency to focus myopically on technical skills. It's so obvious that specific technical capabilities are needed that we focus on them to the exclusion of other skills. As Jeffrey Polzer writes: "This is a sensible starting point because, for example, a software development team cannot work very well without programmers who know the particular coding language to be used in the project; nor can an orchestra succeed without individually talented musicians."[2] Unfortunately, this attention to technical skills often overshadows attention to interpersonal and organizational skills, which, in the long run, may be just as important. For instance, a brilliant programmer may actually retard team progress if she is secretive about her work, is unwilling to collaborate, or generates hostility among other members. In contrast, a person with average technical skills but superb organizational savvy may be the team's most valuable member, thanks to his ability to gather resources, enlist help from the operating units, and so forth.

Polzer cautions that there is still plenty of room for the talented individual contributor who isn't very good at working with others. The person's interpersonal weaknesses may be addressed through coaching or other means. This advice should encourage managers to be sanguine about the positive and negative characteristics of potential team members. Individuals who are strong on all four skill measures—technical, problem-solving, interpersonal, and organizational—are few and far between. Thus, one of the goals of member selection must be to make the most of the talent available and to take steps to neutralize people's weaknesses.

Most experts on team creation caution that you'll rarely get all the skills you need on the team. Something will always be missing. And in most cases, it is impossible to anticipate every skill needed. As researchers Jon Katzenbach and Douglas Smith note: "No team succeeds without all the skills needed to meet its purpose and performance goals. Yet most teams figure out the skill they will need *after* [our emphasis] they are formed."[3] Thus, the savvy team leader looks for people with both valued skills and the potential to learn new ones as needed.

ADDING AND SUBTRACTING MEMBERS. Be prepared to add new members and possibly bid thanks and good-bye to others over time. New skills and members may be needed as the work changes and the team makes progress toward its goal. Consider the example of a process-reengineering team that was charged with redesigning a company's entire customer service function. This team began as a small core group of five members. Over the six months of its life, it recruited five additional members—each representing one of the company's product groups. Once this team completed the plan for customer service redesign, it moved to an implementation stage. At that point, still more people were recruited—people who would play major roles in plan implementation.

One caution on adding and offloading members: Over time, members adjust to the people and the working styles represented on the team. They develop effective patterns for making decisions and communicating—and sometimes do so very gradually. They identify the team with the other players. This cohesion is undermined when too many people join and exit the team. Newcomers are not fully productive during the time they spend getting oriented. Those who remain must expend lots of valuable time orienting the new members and finding ways to work with them; they must spend still more time finding ways to fill in for departed team members. So, minimize this turnover as much as possible.

How Many Is Too Many?

The optimal size for a project team depends on the project's goals and tasks. Thus, the best advice about how many people to have on a team is this: Have just enough people to do the job and no more. Having too few people will slow you down and possibly mean that you don't have all the requisite skills. Having too many will also slow you down by shifting valuable time and energy into communication and coordination efforts. There is also the problem of commitment. Individual commitment to the team and its goals tends to diminish as more people are added. So recruit as many people as you need to get the job done—but no more.

Authors Jon Katzenbach and Douglas Smith offer these cues to knowing whether your team is small enough:[a]

• Team can convene easily and frequently.

• Members can communicate easily and frequently.

• No additional people are required to get the job done.

[a] Jon R. Katzenbach and Douglas K. Smith, *The Wisdom of Teams* (Boston: Harvard Business School Press, 1993), 62.

Team Members' To-Do List

• Complete all assigned tasks on time.

• Communicate dissatisfactions and concerns with the leader and other members.

• Support the leader and other members.

• Help others when they ask, and ask for help when you need it.

RECRUITING. Once a candidate for membership has been identified, his or her potential contribution should be discussed by the team and with the sponsor. The candidate's supervisor should also be consulted, as team membership absorbs time that the candidate would otherwise spend on regular assignments. Assuming agreement among all parties, the candidate can then be invited to join.

Note: The appendixes at the end of this book contain worksheets that can help you as you form your team.

The Project Steering Committee

Some projects have another level of oversight and authority, one we haven't mentioned in our who's who list, called the *project steering committee*. In figure 2-1, this steering committee occupies the box otherwise occupied by the sponsor. In fact, in projects with steering committees, the sponsor is a member of the committee, along with all other key stakeholders. The role of the committee is to do the following:

- Approve the project charter

- Secure resources

- Adjudicate all requests to change key project elements, including deliverables, schedule, and budget

The project steering committee has the ultimate authority on those matters. A steering committee is a good idea when a number of different partnering companies, units, or individuals have a strong stake in the project. A steering committee represents these different interests. As such, it is well positioned to sort out complicated, interfirm, or interdepartment project problems. Likewise, steering committees are valuable when many change requests—concerning deliverables, schedule, and budget—are anticipated.

The downside of having a steering committee is that it involves another level of oversight and that its meetings take up the time of some of the company's most expensive employees. So, don't have a steering committee if you don't need one.

Characteristics of Effective
Project Teams

Aside from the particular skills that people bring to a project, what else should you look for? The literature on team-based work provides some insights.[4] That literature points to several qualities as ingredients in team or project success. They are:

- Competence

- A clear and common goal

- Commitment to the common goal

- An environment within which everyone contributes and everyone benefits

- A supportive structure

- Alignment of project goals with organizational goals

Let's look at each in detail.

Competence

To succeed, the team should have all the talent, knowledge, organizational clout, experience, and technical know-how needed to get the job done. Any weak or missing competencies jeopardize the team goal. In these cases, teams must strengthen weaknesses or recruit for the missing competencies—something that successful teams learn to do as they move forward.

What you need are individuals who bring critical competencies to the effort. As a practical matter, that advice may need to be tempered by the political realities of the organization. For example, Susan's goodwill could be extremely important if she was in a position to block the team's progress. Making her a team member could have the effect of getting her to buy in to team objectives, thus neutralizing her danger to the team.

A Clear, Common Goal

Have you ever been part of a team or project group that didn't have a clear idea of its purpose? If you have, you probably understand why these groups are rarely successful. It is nearly impossible to succeed when team members cannot articulate a clear and common goal. The situation is even worse when the executives who sponsor and charter teams are unclear or uncertain about what they want done.

One way to test for a clear and common goal is to try the "elevator speech" test. Take each member of the project aside and ask the following question: If you were traveling by elevator between the first and second floors with our CEO and he asked what your team was working on, what would you say? Everyone working on the project should be able to clearly and succinctly explain the goal to the CEO—or to any intelligent stranger. Here are two statements that meet the elevator speech test:

- "We are redesigning our Web site with three objectives in mind: to make it capable of accommodating each of our different product groups, to make site updating and expansion faster and less costly, and to enhance the customer experience."

- "We are reengineering the entire customer service process. If we are successful, 95 percent of incoming customer calls will be handled by a single service rep, and 80 percent of all calls will be resolved in three minutes or less."

Can everyone on your team articulate the project's goal with this degree of succinctness and clarity? Would everyone's description of the goal be the same? If you said no to either question, you have a problem. Try to address that problem as a group. As will be explained later, a project's goal is generally handed to it by higher management, which sees a problem or opportunity and wants it dealt with. Ideally, management identifies the end but leaves the means to people on the team. Still, team members must share an understanding of the goal. Otherwise, they will head in different directions, dissipating both energy and resources. Conflict and bickering are guaranteed.

Once they reach a common understanding of the goal, project team members, in concert with management, should specify it in terms of performance metrics. In the example of customer service reengineering, the team specified its goal as follows: "Ninety-five percent of incoming customer calls will be handled by a single service rep, and 80 percent of all calls will be resolved in three minutes or less." Metrics like these not only specify the goal more completely, they also provide a way to gauge progress toward goal completion. For example, this team could have set up interim milestones such as these:

- Within six months, 50 percent of incoming customer calls will be handled by a single rep.

- Within nine months, 75 percent of incoming customer calls will be handled by a single rep.

- Within twelve months, 95 percent of incoming customer calls will be handled by a single rep.

A team without performance metrics cannot determine whether it has been successful.

Commitment to a Common Goal

A shared understanding of the goal is extremely important, but really effective teams go a step further. Their members are committed to the goal. There is a big difference between understanding and commitment. Understanding assures that people know the direction in which they should work; commitment is a visceral quality that motivates them to do the work and to keep working when the going gets tough.

People must see their team's goal as being very important and worthy of effort. If they lack a compelling purpose, some members will not subordinate their personal goals to the team's goal. They will not identify with the team or its purpose.

Commitment is also a function of goal ownership and mutual accountability. Consider the following example:

A number of individuals from different functional areas of a company were brought together to solve a critical problem: Their company was losing customers to a rival that provided the same service at a markedly lower price. That lower price was a function of the rival's greater efficiency in delivering its service. The only solution was to find a way to provide customers with greater value: a lower price, measurably better service, or a combination of the two.

Every member of the project team understood the importance of the goal. Their economic futures and those of their coworkers depended on their success. And because management had not told team members how they should achieve their goal, they had a sense of ownership for both the effort and the result—and held each other accountable for that result.

That's commitment. Don't confuse shared commitment with social compatibility. It's less important that people get along with each other than it is that they are willing to work together to get things done. Having a purpose that all see as important can overcome social incompatibilities.

You can recognize shared commitment in the vocabulary used by team members. When people use *we, us,* and *our* instead of *I, you,* and *they,* team commitment is in the air. Statements like these suggest real teamwork:

- "*We* are making good progress, but each of *us* must pick up the pace."

- "Where do *we* stand with respect to *our* schedule?"

- "*Our* plan is still in the formative stages."

- "Give *us* three months and access to the customer data, and *we'll* develop a workable plan."

Commitment to a common goal is more easily achieved if the number of team members is small. That seems intuitive. The military, among others, has long recognized the importance of small-group cohesion in generating individual commitment to both the unit and its goals. Soldiers will gripe endlessly about the "damned army" but will often risk life and limb for the well-being of their small unit and its members. For this reason, some experts on teams recommend keeping membership as small as possible, with fewer members being better if all the right competencies are represented.

Commitment is also enhanced through rewards. If people understand that promotions, bonuses, or pay increases are associated with their success in achieving the team goal, their commitment will increase. If they understand that the boss will get the credit and the bulk of the monetary rewards, their commitment will evaporate.

Every Member Contributes—Every Member Benefits

Have you ever been on a rowing team? If you have, you know that every member of the team must pull his or her oar with the same intensity and at the same pace as everyone else. There is no room for slackers or for people who won't keep the right pace. Work teams are very similar. Performance depends on everyone contributing— pulling for the goal. Individual members who simply show up at meetings to render their opinions but do no work impair performance and demoralize the active teammates. If team membership has any value, it must be earned through real work. In other words, free riders—team members who obtain the benefits of membership without doing their share—cannot be tolerated.

Not every member must put in the same amount of time on team activities or make the same contribution. Variable contributions to projects are a fact of life. A senior manager, for example, may be a regular team member even though he must direct much of his attention to other duties. He may support the project by securing resources or by building support for the team within the organization. While some people might not see this contribution as real work, it is nevertheless important to the team effort.

There is also the very real fact that some people are a lot more capable and productive than others are, since skill levels are bound to be different. The field of information technology, in particular, includes people with vastly disparate skill levels. So don't become obsessed with free riding.

The team leader must also do real work. He or she cannot be a team member *and* behave like a traditional boss, delegating all the work to others. Thus, there is a certain element of role ambiguity for the team leader, who must wear a leadership cap some of the time and a team member's cap the rest.

And just as each member must contribute to the team's work, each should receive clear benefits. Benefits can take many forms: the psychological reward of doing interesting and meaningful work, a learning experience that will pay future career dividends, or a fatter paycheck. In the absence of clear benefits, individuals will not contribute at a high level—at least not for long; the benefits they derive from their regular jobs will absorb their attention and make team duties a secondary priority.

A Supportive Environment

No project team operates in a vacuum. The project is a small organization embedded within a larger environment of operating units and functional departments. It depends on its organizational kin to one degree or another for resources, information, and assistance. The extent to which operating units and departments are supportive, indifferent, or hostile to the project and its goals is bound to have an impact on the project team's effectiveness. In particular, the team builder needs to consider these environmental factors:

- **Leadership support**.   Support at the top is essential. It assures a source of resources and helps recruit the right people. Leadership support also provides protection from powerful managers and departments that for one reason or another are inclined to torpedo the team effort. One way to secure and keep leadership support is to create what Steven Wheelwright and Kim Clark have eloquently described as "heavyweight teams"—that is, teams headed by people with powerful skills and abundant organizational clout.[5]

- **A nonhierarchical structure**.   Team-based work is more likely to be successful if the organization does not conform to a rigid hierarchical structure. Why? Because a nonhierarchical structure creates habits that are conducive to team-based work—specifically, a willingness to share information, collaboration across organizational boundaries, and employee empowerment. These habits are weak or absent in organizations where the bosses do all the thinking and directing and everyone else follows orders. Such organizations are not team-ready.

- **Appropriate reward systems**. Companies that are new to team-based work need to examine their reward systems before launching teams; they must find a different balance in rewards for individual and team-based success. Doing so is one of the most daunting challenges faced by those who sponsor teams.

- **Experience with team-based work**. Teams benefit when their companies and individual members have plenty of experience with team-based work. Experience provides insights into what works and what does not, how best to organize around a goal, how to collaborate, and how to alter the team at different points in its life cycle. Many companies that rely on team-based work provide training on team methods, and with good reason. Employees who've worked independently for years must be trained in team-based work. Specifically, they need help with skills such as listening, communicating with different kinds of people, collaborating with people outside their departments, and staying focused on the common task.

How supportive of team-based work is your organization? Your organization's team-readiness should factor into your decision to attack a problem or opportunity through a team.

Alignment

Alignment is the last item on our list of essentials for project team effectiveness. It refers to the coordination of plans, effort, and rewards with an organization's highest goals. In an aligned organization, everyone understands both the goals of the enterprise and the goals of his or her operating unit. In an aligned organization, people work in the right direction—and the rewards system encourages them to do so.

Project teams also need alignment. A team shouldn't even exist unless it represents the best way to help the organization achieve its goals. So, the goals of the project team should align with organizational goals, and the goals of individual team members should align—through the team—with those higher organizational goals. And everyone's efforts should align through the rewards system. This last point is very important, and it begins at the top, with the sponsor. Since the sponsor is accountable for team success, some part of his or her compensation should be linked to the team's performance. Moving down the line, the team's leader and members should likewise see their compensation affected by team outcomes.

Alignment gets everyone moving in the same direction—the right direction.

Summing Up

- A project sponsor authorizes the project, defines the scope of the work, provides resources, and accepts or rejects the final output.

- The project manager receives authority from the sponsor and plays a central role in each phase of the project's life cycle.

- A project team leader reports to the project manager and takes responsibility for one or more aspects of the work.

- Members of the project team do most of the work. They should be selected on the basis of their skills and ability to collaborate effectively with others.

- A team should have just enough people to do the job and no more.

- Successful teams have these characteristics: competence, a clear and compelling goal, commitment to the common goal, an environment within which everyone contributes and everyone benefits, a supportive environment, and alignment of project goals with organizational goals.

3

A Written Charter

Your Marching Orders

Key Topics Covered in This Chapter

- *The value of a project charter*

- *Eight things a charter should contain*

- *The problem of ends and means*

- *How to scope a project*

WE'VE ALREADY established the importance of having a clear objective. Having that objective defined, specified, and delivered in written form is very important. But the project team needs more than a clearly stated goal to do its work. It needs an unambiguous sense of the project's scope, the value it should deliver to stakeholders, the time frame within which it must work, and a statement of the resources at its disposal. Together, these constitute the charter that authorizes the project and defines its activities—the subject of this chapter.

A Mandate for Action

Having the right cast of characters on a project team is important. But so is having a *charter* that spells out the nature and scope of the work and management's expectations for results. A charter is a concise written document containing some or all of the following:

- Name of project's sponsor

- Relationship between the project's goals and higher organizational goals

- The benefits of the project to the organization

- The expected time frame of the work

- A concise description of project deliverables (objectives)

- The budget, allocations, and resources available to the project team

- The project manager's authority

- The sponsor's signature

Without a formal charter, the project could head off in a direction that is misaligned with organizational objectives. It could grow in scope without control, a process known as "mission creep." The very act of creating a charter forces senior management to clearly articulate what the project should do—an important duty when senior management is not of one mind, as in this example:

Phil was the sponsor of the company's effort to reengineer its order-fulfillment and customer service operations. As an outspoken critic of these functions, he was the right person for the job. He had long been dissatisfied with the time it took to fill orders and with the company's unspectacular level of customer service. In addition, he thought the costs of these operations were too high. So he put Lila in charge of a project effort to improve them.

What sorts of cost cutting was Phil anticipating? What exactly were his complaints about the current system? What would success look like? Lila attempted to pin Phil down on those questions, but without success. He was too busy to think it all through and too eager to delegate responsibility for the project's outcome. Other company executives were also anxious to see improvements but, like Phil, had no clear ideas about the outcomes they wanted. So when Lila quizzed senior managers about the subject, they cited no specific goals. Lacking clear guidance, Lila and the people on her team developed their own goals and criteria for success.

The team pushed forward, and Lila reported progress to Phil over the course of the ten-month effort. Resources were always a problem, particularly since Lila was never sure how much money she could spend and how many people she could bring on to the team at key stages. Every request for resources had to be negotiated on a case-by-case basis with Phil.

The team eventually completed its tasks, meeting all of its self-declared goals. It had cut order-fulfillment time by one-third. Ninety percent of customers could now get all their issues resolved with a single phone call.

And the overall cost of these functions had been cut by 12 percent. The project team celebrated the completion of its duties with a splendid dinner, after which its members went back to their regular duties.

Senior management, however, was not entirely pleased with the outcome. "You did a pretty good job," Phil told Lila. "The improvements you've made are significant, but we were looking for a more sweeping reorganization and larger cost savings." Lila was stunned and more than slightly angry. "If he wanted these things," she thought, "why didn't he say so?"

Situations like Lila's are common but can be avoided through a charter. Does your project have a written charter? Does it contain each of the important elements?

Clarify Objectives

As Lila's case demonstrates, project managers need more than a broad-brush description of the objectives for which they will be responsible. Ambiguity on the goals can lead to misunderstandings, disappointment, and expensive rework. Consider this example of a broad-brush objective: "Develop a Web site that's capable of providing fast, accurate, cost-effective product information and fulfillment to our customers." That is how a sponsor might describe the project's objective in the charter. But what exactly does it mean? What is "fast"? How should accuracy be defined? Is one error in 1,000 transactions acceptable, or would one error in 10,000 meet the sponsor's expectations? To what

---

Tip on Setting Objectives

When defining project objectives, think SMART. In other words, be sure that objectives are: Specific, Measurable, Action-oriented, Realistic, and Time-limited.

SOURCE: Harvard ManageMentor® on Project Management.

degree must the site be cost effective? Each of those questions should be answered in consultation with the sponsor and key stakeholders.

A thoughtful charter indicates the ends but does not specify the means. The means should be left to the project manager, team leader, and members. Doing otherwise—that is, telling the team what it should do *and* how to do it—would undermine any benefit derived from having recruited a competent team. Richard Hackman makes this point clear in his book *Leading Teams*. "Direction that is unclear or extremely abstract," he writes, "can waste members' time and embroil them in conflicts as they struggle to agree on what they are really supposed to do. Direction that is *too* clear and complete, on the other hand, can lessen members' commitment to the work and sometimes prompts unwanted and even unethical behaviors." Per Hackman, the sponsor must find a balance between giving the team too much and too little specific direction.[1] As he makes clear in figure 3-1, teams do best when the ends are specified and the means are not (upper-right quadrant), when they do goal-oriented work and manage themselves. As he writes: "When ends are specified but

FIGURE 3-1

Means and Ends

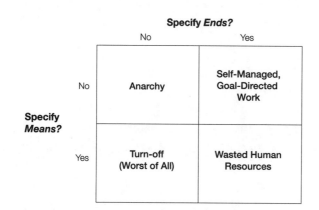

Source: J. Richard Hackman, *Leading Teams* (Boston: Harvard Business School Press, 2002), 73.
Reproduced with permission.

means are not, team members are able to—indeed, are implicitly encouraged to—draw on their full complement of knowledge, skill, and experience in devising and executing a way of operating that is well tuned to the team's purpose and circumstances."[2] This is not to say that specifying *both* ends and means (lower-right quadrant) will necessarily lead to failure. That situation more closely describes a traditional, unempowered, work group.

Make It Time–Bound

All objectives should be specific and measurable. If they are not, you'll have no way of knowing whether the project has met its goals. There should also be a time frame within which objectives will be achieved; the project cannot be open-ended. In some cases, the deadline must be firm: a situation with a fixed time and variable scope. For example, in sending a probe to Mars in the summer of 2003, a project team at NASA had a limited window of opportunity. Mars and Earth were in unusually close proximity at that time. By late August, the distances between them would begin to increase rapidly. NASA had to launch its Martian explorer in July or scrub the project. With time as a constraint, the agency had to be flexible about the scope of the space vehicle it was putting together.

Some projects define time as a constant. Consider a software company that decides that it will deliver a new release every three months. Since time is constant, the project team must make adjustments to the scope of its new releases—adding or dropping product features—to assure that each can be delivered at the end of three months.

The opposite situation is evident in situations with a fixed scope and variable time. As we'll see later in this book, if the scope of the project is set, then a logical deadline can only be established after the project manager and team have had an opportunity to break down each objective into a set of tasks and then estimate the duration of each of those tasks. Nevertheless, the charter should contain a reasonable deadline—one that can be amended as the project team learns more about what it must do.

Be Specific About Project Scope

Even with a charter in hand, the project manager and key players must spell out the project scope in greater detail. One useful technique for scoping a project is to have key stakeholders and project participants join in a brainstorming exercise that specifically aims to describe what should be within the scope of the project and what should not. Consider this example:

Amalgamated Hat Rack, Inc. had a problem. Its inventory costs were unacceptably high and growing relative to sales. "We now offer twenty different models of hat and coat racks," the chief operating officer complained at a meeting with managers from purchasing, product development, manufacturing, and inventory control, "and most of them use unique sets of parts."

"That's right," said, Ralph, the inventory manager. "Every time we design a new rack, it incorporates many fittings and fasteners that are not common to our other products. As a result, I now have more than 300 different parts and materials in the stockroom, every one of which must be tracked and stored. Some of them sit there for years. And that's expensive."

The purchasing manager cited another dimension of the problem. "Storage and tracking isn't the only issue. Buying small volumes of many different parts creates paperwork costs for my department and eliminates most of our opportunities for high-volume orders from suppliers—the kinds of orders that produce large discounts."

Everyone agreed that controlling inventory costs was an important goal for the company, and just about everyone at the meeting had an idea for dealing with it. The question was, How could the group define the scope of the project to rein in costs without agreeing to more objectives than they could reasonably tackle? The COO asked Ralph, the inventory manager, to recruit a project team and find a way.

Within two weeks, Ralph had recruited six key people to the team and convened a three-hour meeting to brainstorm the challenge of high inventory costs. The COO and a key parts supplier were invited to participate. Each had a different perspective on the problem. Together they tried to determine what should be within the scope of the project and what should not. Table 3-1 contains the output of their discussion.

The example in table 3-1 demonstrates how a team can define the scope of a project and how it can eliminate activities that would dissipate energy and resources. Notice that the team removed two product design proposals from the project's scope even though those

TABLE 3-1

Amalgamated Defines Project Scope

GOAL: REDUCE INVENTORY COSTS		
Within the Project's Scope	***Not* Within the Project's Scope**	**Comments**
Determine the cost savings of reducing the total number of parts by 25%.		"Reducing total number of parts will reduce our storage and tracking costs and reduce complexity. We should know how much."
	Benchmark current inventory costs against key competitors.	"That would take too much time. Besides, we don't have to know what our competitors are doing in order to achieve significant reductions."
	Develop a plan to design parts complexity out of future products.	"A great idea, but should be a separate project run by the product development people."
Develop an approved parts list (with opportunities for exceptions when necessary) from which product developers can pick. Estimate the cost savings from such a procedure.		"Most of our fasteners are invisible to customers. There's no reason we cannot design new products from a smaller set of these parts."
	Reengineer our new-product design process.	"A good idea, but it deserves to be a separate project."
Develop a plan for just-in-time parts delivery.		"This will save us on floor space and inventory carrying costs. We should have done this years ago."

ideas had considerable merit. Each would make a worthwhile project in itself, but both were judged to be outside the immediate scope of the current project. This determination demonstrates how project managers, members, and sponsors must make trade-offs among the options they discover. Options are always more numerous than available time and resources.

If the sponsor's expectation specifies the ends to be sought, the project plan specifies the means in actionable terms. The project plan may be the project manager's creation. Ideally, it will represent the best ideas of many, or of all, project team members. With the sponsor's approval, this plan becomes part two of the charter.

A project plan is especially useful for large, complex endeavors because it provides more detail about tasks, milestones, deliverables, risks, and timetables. It serves as a road map, both for the team and other interested parties.

Note: Need a handy tool to help you think through the scope of your project? Appendix A contains a "Defining Your Project" worksheet that will take you through key questions you need to answer.

Summing Up

- A project charter is a mandate for action. It spells out in writing the nature and scope of the work and the sponsor's expectations for results.

- A charter should be unambiguous. Make it specific, measurable, action-oriented, realistic, and time-bound.

- When you develop a charter, spell out the ends, but leave the means to the project team.

- Specify what is within the scope of the project and what is not.

4

A Framework for Action

Important First Steps

Key Topics Covered in This Chapter

- *Reaching agreement on how decisions will be made*

- *A method for keeping track of unresolved issues*

- *A procedure for documenting decisions and actions*

- *A plan for communicating*

- *Creating a budget*

LIKE OTHER important ventures, a project moves along more smoothly if certain procedures and operational mechanisms are established before the real work begins. How will decisions be made? How will project participants stay in touch and keep up-to-date? How will unresolved issues be handled? This chapter addresses a number of these organizational issues. Get them in order and everything else will go more smoothly. And determine the rules at the very beginning. You don't want to be making them up as you go along.

Decisions, Decisions

Experienced project managers know that decisions are a major part of their work. Every project is, in fact, a set of activities linked together by decisions. Thus, one of the important things that must be done very early is to agree on (1) how decisions will be made and (2) who will make them. If members lack consensus, the project will find itself tied up in knots. The project manager—or the sponsor—may find every little decision parked on his or her desk. Alternatively, the project will either waste a lot of time in unproductive debate or produce decisions that many stakeholders will not support. And decisions like these are waiting around every corner:

Should one minor goal be traded off for another?

Three alternative new product designs are on the table. The design team must select one.

Which consultant should the team hire, and what should be the scope of the consulting engagement?

The strategy team is overspending its budget. Which activities should be cut?

The team is receiving a lot of change requests from product groups, and they are very good ideas. Adopting them will put the team behind schedule and over budget, but it might be worth it. Can the team make this decision, or must it defer to the steering committee?

Within functional business units, decisions are the domain of executives and managers. These individuals identify the issue, seek out and analyze alternatives, and take counsel from appropriate sources. They then make decisions and accept responsibility for the consequences. Decision making within their own scopes of responsibility is one of the things that managers and executives are paid to do. Though they may seek consensus and the input of others, they are not bound by others' opinions. Project teams must approach decisions differently.

Decision–Making Spheres

Project decision making is not as clear cut as decision making within operating units or staff departments. Sponsors and steering committees obviously have decision-making authority over team goals and the level of resources allocated to the team. They also maintain ultimate authority on

- personnel;

- expenditures over a given budget amount;

- bringing in outside resources;

- changes in organization-wide policy or goals;

- choices affecting customers, such as pricing and specifications; and

- changes in the team's deliverables and schedule.

But even they must recognize the views of key stakeholders, who may demand a voice in these decisions.

Project managers, on the other hand, should have sole authority over decisions related to project operations and processes as long as they do nothing to

- alter the goal or deliverable,

- adversely affect the schedule, or

- adversely affect the budget.

The same applies to team leaders and team members. These participants need the authority to make decisions within their limited spheres *unless* their decisions will have comparable negative effects or impact the work of other project teams.

To avoid potential disagreements, be sure that your project team, its sponsor, key stakeholders, and higher management have a shared understanding of which decisions can be made by the different players and groups associated with the project.

Decision Procedures Matter

Research indicates that people care about decision procedures. They want protocol to be fair. And they are much more likely to accept a decision that is unfavorable to them as long as they believe the procedure for making the decision was fair. Trust is a key element in this phenomenon. People must trust those who devise the decision-making procedure. If they see others rigging it and acting out of self-interest, then their willingness to accept decisions—and their commitment to the project—will evaporate.

The Who and How of Decisions

If you are a project manager or a team leader, you must help others agree on the who and how of decision making. Who will make the decisions? At the team level, will the team leader or a subset of team members make decisions, or will all members have a voice? How will decisions be made? Will the majority rule, or must the group reach a full consensus? Will decisions be final? If not, what kind of modification process will the team follow?

Here are some common decision-making approaches:

- **Majority rule**. Participants bring their input to the meeting, discuss, and then vote. Decisions that receive more than 50 percent of the votes are adopted.

- **Consensus**. Every member of the team must agree before a decision can be made and adopted. If consensus cannot be reached, new alternatives must be developed and brought back to the group.

- **Small group decides**. A group of individuals with relevant experience and skills is selected to make decisions.

- **Leader decides with input**. The team leader gathers input from team members and then makes the decision.

In selecting a decision-making approach, participants should weigh the trade-offs. The more involved the team members are in the decision-making process, the more likely it is that they will support the outcome. As a result, the consensus and majority-rules approaches can help build team commitment. But there is a downside: Those methods take time. If time is an important issue, the team might consider using different approaches in different situations: It could reach an agreement collectively on issues that are most important to members and use a more streamlined approach for the rest.

Whichever choices are made about decision making, establishing them during the project's start-up stage is extremely important. Failing to agree on the decision rules will only lead to bickering and dissention. If time and events indicate that those rules are not supporting key goals, change them in an orderly manner.

Tracking and Disposing of Unresolved Issues

How many meetings have you attended during which important issues were raised but not resolved? Probably plenty. Even when there is a consensus that certain issues are important, many are left on the table. Why? Because you've run out of time. Or because participants didn't have sufficient information to form an opinion. Or some individuals needed to give the subject more thought. Those are all valid reasons for deferring the resolution of issues. The question is, What happens to issues that you cannot resolve in the course of project work or meetings? Are they forgotten? Stuffed into a drawer? Sent into orbit? Unresolved issues can clog up the decision pipeline if there isn't an orderly and systematic way of dealing with them. They can also hold up project work if a certain task must wait for a decision before moving forward.

One way to deal with unresolved issues is to enter them into a tracking log. A tracking log has two benefits: (1) unresolved issues will not be lost and (2) a procedure for their timely resolution will be assured. Table 4-1 is just one of many possible versions of tracking logs.

TABLE 4-1

Tracking Log Example

Issue	First Raised	By (Owner)	Comments	Must Resolve By
Selection of materials supplier	3/03/04	A. Sandoval	Holding three bids	5/21/04
Find new tech team leader	3/07/04	K. McIntyre	Current leader will retire on 5/13/04	ASAP
Whether to attend the June 2004 APRQ conference	3/10/04	J. Johnson	Cost not yet calculated. Deadline for application is 4/18/04	4/16/04

Simply creating a log does not eliminate the problem of unresolved issues. Someone simply takes responsibility for them and for bringing them back to the decision forum in a timely way. Both the issue owners and the project manager should share that responsibility—owners because they are the ones who contend that their issues are important, and the project manager because he or she shapes the agenda.

The important point—and the benefit of using a tracking log—is that the issues that matter won't be lost or forgotten.

Documenting Decisions and Actions

If you participate in several meetings each day, you probably know how easy it is to lose track of what decisions are made in those meetings, and who is assigned various post-meeting action steps. Confusion follows.

"I never agreed to that plan. What I did agree to was . . . ."

"As we decided several months ago, the supplier pool will be limited to the three companies with whom we have been dealing. John, why the puzzled look? Don't you remember that agreement?"

"So we've now shared our plan with each of the affected departments and their personnel. We did meet with each of them, didn't we?"

Do those statements and questions sound familiar? If they do, you need a method for keeping track of the decisions made by your group. Minutes and progress reports can serve this purpose.

Minutes

A sizable project with plenty of meetings and many participants can easily lose track of what has been done, and what hasn't—who agreed to do what, and who did not. This is why all but the smallest projects should have a systematic method for keeping track of decisions, assignments, and actions.

Many organizations use meeting minutes—notes recorded by an appointed individual—for this purpose. The minutes are reviewed and approved at the next meeting, with amendments made if necessary. Those approved minutes then go into a file, where participants can consult them as needed.

Progress Reports

Minutes are useful and should be taken at every high-level meeting. Simple notes will suffice at lower-level ones. But meetings are not the only forums in which decisions and actions are taken. For every hour that people spend in meetings, many hours of work are being done elsewhere—at least one would hope so! For example, to support a project team that's working on a new product line, people in an R&D lab are busy testing materials and component interfaces. Marketing specialists are surveying potential customers about their needs. Financial analysts are crunching numbers, trying to estimate costs and the value of the new product line to the company. Each of those activities should report progress and problems to the project manager, who must digest the information and use it to track the progress of the project as a whole.

Which reports are needed should be determined by the situation and by the information that the project manager requires to maintain control and move the effort forward. Like meeting minutes, progress reports should be filed in an orderly way that makes them accessible to whoever needs the information they contain. The specifications of the filing system are less important than the consistency and transparency of the system itself.

Note: The appendixes at the end of this book contain a form you can use or adapt for your progress reports.

Creating a Communications Plan

A communications plan is one of the other things that must be created at the front end of project work. The importance of such a plan is a function of the number of people, departments, and entities that will participate—and their geographic dispersal. Small projects that involve a handful of colocated people may not need a plan, except for a regularly scheduled meeting time and place. These people can share information anytime they walk down the hallway or go into the coffee room. In contrast, a large project that brings together dozens of people from many departments, various geographic locations, and different organizations must have a highly structured and complete communications plan. Getting these widely scattered people to talk with one another and share ideas will be challenging. Thus, an infrastructure for communicating must be put in place. Without it, participants in a major project will not be able to coordinate their efforts, resolve problems, and hit target delivery dates.

Tips for Communicating Within Larger Projects

If yours is a large project, chances are that its working participants will be scattered around the building. Some may be located at company facilities in other cities or other countries. A few may not even be company employees, but suppliers or employees of a strategic partner. How can you communicate information easily to these people as needed? And how can you help them communicate with each other? Here are a few tips:

- Give a competent person responsibility for creating a project Web site and Web-based newsletter, especially if the time line for completion is long. Use the newsletter to report progress, problems, and upcoming events.

- Use the project Web site to post the charter, assignments, meeting dates, meeting minutes, and other material. People can access that information on a self-serve basis.

- Bundle the e-mail addresses of each work group. Chances are that your e-mail software has a group feature that allows you to send a message to a predetermined set of individuals with a single click. That functionality makes it easy to send information to the people who need it without bothering everyone else with needless e-mail.

Every project communications plan should include protocols for meetings, e-mail, and reporting. Larger projects should consider a project team room and electronic linkages—such as a project Web site, phone conferencing, and videoconferencing—that are capable of connecting widely dispersed stakeholders and team members.

Meetings

Projects are punctuated by meetings. Regularly scheduled meetings. On-the-fly meetings. Meetings that deal with emergencies.

Meetings are the *least* favorite activity of busy, action-oriented people but are often the best way to communicate information. Meetings also provide forums within which ideas can be shared and decisions can be made; progress generally depends on those decisions. Thus, if your project must have meetings, and plenty of them, it's smart to make the most of them.

At one level, making the most of meetings involves sticking to a regular schedule as much as possible. If people know that project team meetings take place every Monday from 3 to 4 P.M., for example, they can plan their other responsibilities around those days and times. Having a regular schedule also saves meeting organizers the time-consuming task of finding a time on which many people can agree.

Attendance Policies

There should also be an attendance policy associated with project meetings. Decisions cannot be made when key players are not at the table. Instead, decisions must be deferred to the next scheduled meeting, creating havoc with scheduled work in the process.

The problem of meeting absenteeism is particularly acute when key project participants retain considerable responsibility for their regular jobs. For example, if the company controller is required to spend 85 percent of her time on her regular job, her participation in project meetings will take a backseat to other demands on her time—unless there is a policy about attending. So establish a policy at the outset. If travel is an impediment to meeting attendance, consider using telecommunication technology to link travelers to meetings as they happen. More on this in just a bit.

Note: Making the most of meetings involves preparation, engaging the right processes during the meeting, and following up on the decisions and agreements made. If you'd like to learn about these aspects of meetings, see "A Guide to Effective Meetings" in Appendix B. This guide will help you to prepare for and conduct your meetings, and to follow up effectively.

Meeting Technology

There are times when e-mails won't do—when team members simply must get together to talk about their work. In some cases, the ability to communicate verbally is sufficient. In others, people must also be able to see each other or the physical objects that others are working on: a person who has just joined the team, a prototype, or four different color choices for a new product. Sometimes, they may want to see how a customer has adapted a product to make it more effective. Fortunately, we now have plenty of affordable technologies that make each of those different forms of communication possible.

E-MAIL. E-mail is a remarkable communications tool. Messages can be transmitted almost instantly and at a very low cost from one part of the building to another, or across thousands of miles. Word-processing files, photos, scanned documents, and presentation slides can be attached and transmitted at almost the same heart-stopping speed.

Every project member should have an e-mail address and the addresses of all other participants. If you plan to rely heavily on e-mailing attached documents, check for compatibility and compression issues, and establish protocols for use. Be clear about who must be "copied" on what, and don't overdo it. There's probably no need to "cc" every person on the team list with every correspondence you send out; nobody wants to receive massive amounts of irrelevant e-mail. Also make sure that everyone is informed about decisions that affect them and that the people who need to participate in decisions are consulted.

E-mails can help create virtual paper trails and can provide important information down the line if misunderstandings or conflicts arise.

TELEPHONE CONFERENCING. The telephone conference is the quickest and easiest way for the virtual team to communicate verbally. And it has a feature that e-mail lacks: It provides an opportunity for dynamic, give-and-take conversations. That advantage makes teleconferencing a better medium when your goal is to discuss, to brainstorm, to resolve problems, or to make decisions.

Many kinds of teleconferencing technologies are now available. Check with your communications service providers about the most current options.

VIDEOCONFERENCING. Videoconferencing is another channel of project connectivity. It can bring teams together without wasting

---

Visual Trumps Audio

In their valuable article "Distance Matters," Gary Olson and Judith Olson conclude that attempts to use connective technologies either fail or require major efforts by team members to adjust to using the media technologies. Apart from that blanket conclusion, they note that video connections are far superior to audio alone:

> *Our laboratory data show that even for people who know each other and have worked together before, a simple audio connection for conversation and a shared editor for real-time work is insufficient to produce the same quality of work as that done face to face. Those with video connections produced output that was indistinguishable from that produced by people who were face to face. The process of their work changed, however, to require more clarification and more management overhead (discussions about how they will conduct the work, not actually doing the work).*

SOURCE: Gary M. Olson and Judith S. Olson, "Distance Matters," *Human Computer Interactions*, 15 (2000): 152.

time or money on meals, travel, and lodging. Project teams located in London, Paris, and Montreal, for example, can see and interact with their colleagues in Rome without leaving their offices. They can see and discuss the same objects and documents in real time. Videoconferencing, however, is complicated and requires the help of people with specialized technical skills. For basic video, participants need the appropriate computer, camera, microphone, software, and Internet connection. Unfortunately, systems from different vendors aren't always compatible with different computers, so if your team opts for video, be sure everyone gets a compatible system.

Bringing People into Contact

Distance matters in team-based work. The greater the physical proximity between project participants, the more likely they are to interact and share ideas on a regular basis. As MIT researcher Tom Allen discovered years ago: "People are more likely to communicate with those who are located nearest to them. Individuals and groups can therefore be positioned in ways that will either promote or inhibit communication."[1] Thus, the physical locations of project team members have a major impact on the depth of communication and knowledge sharing.

Authors Marc Meyer and Al Lehnerd underscore the importance of colocation in their book on team-based product-platform development.

> *The principles of colocating teams, exposing them to a variety of information, and providing a persistent display of that information, are important. . . . Just bringing team members together into one physical place has been shown to improve communication and information sharing. There, small bits of knowledge and information that by themselves mean nothing can be pieced together with other bits to form meaningful insights. Team colocation also fosters bonding between individual members and the commitment needed for focused, fast, high-risk projects.*[2]

One effective approach to the colocation issue—even when moving team members' individual work spaces into close proximity is not feasible—is establishment of a project *team room*. A team room is a space dedicated to the work of the team and its members. It functions as a space for meetings, as a place where members can congregate to share ideas, and where all the physical artifacts and records of the team's work can be displayed or kept. Those artifacts and records may include the following:

- Disassembled competing products

- The team's current prototypes

- Relevant test and research reports

- A specialized library of technical books and journals

The team room may also post these items on the walls:

- A large Gantt chart that plots the project's schedule and milestones from start to finish

- The original copy of the team charter, signed by the executive sponsor

- The team budget, including current variances

This team room should also be equipped with a speakerphone—and perhaps videoconferencing equipment—to accommodate group discussion with off-site members. A whiteboard and paper flip chart should complete the setting. Collectively, the team room and its accoutrements facilitate team work and foster team identity.

The team room we've just described may not be feasible if project participants are widely scattered in a large office building or across borders. But you can get some of the same benefits by means of a project Web site. A virtual team room can be set up in the project Web site using four walls, like those in a real team room:

- **Purpose wall**. This wall includes the team charter, goals, tasks, a list of deliverables, and current results.

- **People wall**. This section identifies the team members and states their roles. Here, users can find out who is involved with

Tips for Making the Most of Your Team Room

A project team room is the natural setting for meetings. But you'll only get the full benefits of the space if people make it a regular gathering place. Here are a few things you can do to draw people to the team room on a regular basis:

- Sponsor periodic brown-bag luncheons in the team room. Use a particular topic, a visiting research scientist, a key customer, or an executive from an alliance partner as a magnet to bring people together for these informal sessions.

- Create an informal and comfortable space by eliminating traditional meeting-room furniture in favor of sofas, coffee tables, and lounge chairs.

- Keep plenty of drawing pads and pens on hand to encourage people to sketch out their ideas.

- Include a small refrigerator stocked with soda, juice, and snacks, which will draw team members into the room, where they will talk with each other.

different aspects of the project. If possible, attach a photo of each team member and a brief description of his or her particular work and expertise. Putting a face and a bit of history with a name adds an important dimension to virtual team work.

- **Document wall.** This part of the site contains a schedule of upcoming meetings and their agendas. Minutes of past meetings and any meeting presentations are also stored here. Members can use this wall to post their work for review by colleagues. Those reviews and comments can likewise be posted.

- **Communications wall.** This section contains links and information that connect everyone on the team.

Finding Balance in Process Formalization

Everything we've addressed so far has concerned processes for facilitating project work: how decisions will be made, how communication will be maintained, and so forth. Attention to process is important, but don't go overboard. Robert Austin and his coauthors at Harvard Business School advocate a minimalist approach to process formalization. In their view, projects must find a balance between discipline and agility. Formalization of process supports discipline, but it will reduce agility if it adheres excessively to processes. "The companies that have been most successful in balancing discipline and agility," they write, "have neither eschewed process formalization altogether nor let process formalization effort overwhelm them. Rather, they have developed simple process management tools based on the ideas that the best balance is one that includes the minimum formal specification critical to [process success]."

SOURCE: Lynda M. Applegate, Robert D. Austin, and F. Warren McFarlan, *Corporate Information Strategy and Management*, 6th ed. (Burr Ridge, IL: McGraw-Hill/Irwin, 2002), 278.

Web sites are great assets, but they require some tending. Someone must monitor and update the site. Depending on the scope of the project, this important job could even be someone's total contribution to the team.

Developing the Budget

A *budget* is the translation of plans into measurable expenditures and anticipated returns over a certain period of time. In this sense it is the financial blueprint or action plan for the project. For businesses, a good budget can be the difference between success and failure because a good budget—and adherence to it—gives people the resources they need to complete their tasks. Project budgets serve a similar function.

The first question to ask when developing a budget is, What is it going to take—in terms of resources—to successfully complete this project? To determine the project's costs, break it down into the key cost categories you anticipate. Here are the typical categories in which projects generate costs:

- **Personnel**. This is almost always the largest part of a project's budget and includes full-time and temporary workers.

- **Travel**. People may have to shuttle from location to location in the course of their project work. Is everyone on-site, or will the team have to be brought together at one locale? Don't forget to budget for meals and lodging.

- **Training**. Will training be required? If the answer is yes, will that training take place on-site, or will there be travel expenses involved? If you plan to hire an outside contractor to do the training, the budget must reflect his or her fees and expenses.

- **Supplies**. In addition to the usual—computers, pens, papers, and software—you may need unusual equipment. Try to antici-pate what the project will require.

- **Space**. Some people may have to be relocated to rented space. How much room and money will that require?

- **Research and professional service**. Will you have to buy studies or hire a market-research firm? Do you plan to bring in a con-sultant or seek legal advice? The budget must reflect the cost of each of these.

Since costs are estimated before the work actually begins, com-pletion of the budget gives team members a chance to ask them-selves whether they really want to do this project, given the cost. The sponsor, for example, may wish to reconsider the project or re-duce its scope once costs are estimated. Likewise, if the sponsor is unwilling to fully fund the budget, the project manager, and anyone else charged with the success or failure of the effort, may wish to withdraw. Projects that are not fully funded are imperiled from the very beginning.

In some cases, the project budget cannot be flexible. A project governed by a contract with a fixed total payment is just one example. Internally operated projects, however, usually have some flexibility, which is often necessary since it is extremely difficult to anticipate every expense. The best projects, after all, are those that alter themselves as they run into roadblocks and encounter valuable opportunities. It is for that reason that many project managers build some wiggle room into their budgets. They ask for 5 percent or so of the estimated budget for that purpose. The extra allowance gives them a limited ability to deal with unanticipated costs without having to beg the sponsor for additional funding.

Once a project has been launched, the project manager can use the budget to monitor progress by comparing the actual results with the budgeted results. This feedback, or monitoring and evaluation of progress, in turn allows the team to take timely, corrective action.

Summing Up

- Your project will link its many activities with decisions—dozens and dozens of them. So before you get under way, determine who will make the decisions and how. Tactics include majority rule, consensus, small-group decisions, and decision by the official leader.

- During meetings, issues will come up that cannot be resolved then and there. If those issues are important, they must be tracked and brought back to decision makers at an appropriate time. Use a tracking log for this purpose.

- Document decisions as they are made so that people can remember what they've agreed to do.

- Communication is essential in a large, broadly distributed project. Create a workable plan for communicating with project members. And make it easy for them to communicate with each other.

- Colocate project team members to the extent possible. The closer their physical proximity to each other, the greater the communication among them.

- Telecommunications technologies—including project Web sites, e-mail, phone conferencing, and videoconferencing—can provide communications channels for geographically dispersed project teams.

- Create a budget. It will help you stay on track.

5

Work Breakdown

From Huge Job to Manageable Tasks

Key Topics Covered in This Chapter

- *Using work breakdown structure to subdivide complex tasks into many smaller tasks*

- *Estimating time and resource requirements for each task*

- *Fitting people to tasks*

ONCE YOU HAVE completed all the housekeeping processes and set up a budget for your project, you are ready to move into the first area of technique, which aims to decompose a large job into a set of manageable tasks.

Many of the objectives addressed through projects are huge and mind boggling in their complexity. To those of us who don't work in the construction industry, the job of building an eighty-story office building seems impossibly complex. How would you create a foundation capable of carrying the weight of a million tons of steel girders and other materials—all of which must arrive on the site at the right time and in the right order? How would you get elevators and running water to the top-most floors? How would you go about the job of organizing, scheduling, and directing a small army of electricians, steelworkers, plumbers, masons, glaziers, and many others?

Seems incomprehensible, doesn't it? Approaching a project this daunting and of this magnitude is reminiscent of the old joke that asks, "How do you eat an elephant?" Though the challenge is intimidating, the answer is simple and commonsensical: Cut the elephant into bite-sized pieces. The same approach applies to projects large and small—namely, break the objective into a set of manageable tasks. This chapter explains how the concept of *work breakdown structure* (WBS) can be used to do just that. Using WBS, and starting with the top objective, you can decompose the project goal into the many tasks required to achieve it. The time and money needed to complete those tasks can then be estimated. This approach helps project managers answer these key questions:

- What must we do to achieve our goals?

- How long will it take?

- What will it cost?

Many projects fail because a significant part of the work has been overlooked, or because the time required to complete the work has been grossly underestimated. If you are building and installing a new database management system, for example, and forget to include the time and cost of training people on it, you are unlikely to meet all your objectives. But careful scrutiny can save the day. This chapter explains how you can break each objective down into its component tasks and make reasonable estimates for the time and resources necessary to accomplish each task.

Work Breakdown Structure

WBS is a tool that project managers use to develop estimates, assign personnel, track progress, and reveal the scope of project work. You can use this tool to subdivide complex tasks into many smaller tasks. These tasks, in turn, can usually be broken down still further.

To create a WBS, ask this question: What will have to be done in order to accomplish our objective? By asking that same question over and over for each task and subtask, you will eventually reach a point at which tasks cannot be subdivided. Consider this example:

ABC Auto Company plans to introduce a new passenger car. This is a big, big job. At the highest level, its employees are faced with four tasks:

1. Determine customer requirements.

2. Design a vehicle that will meet those requirements.

3. Construct the vehicle.

4. Test the vehicle.

As figure 5-1 indicates, each of those top-level tasks can be broken down into a set of subtasks. And each of the subtasks shown in the

FIGURE 5-1

Work Breakdown Structure for Sample Automobile Project

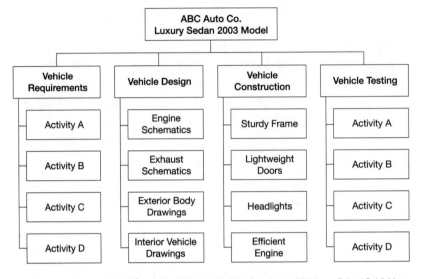

figure can be broken down still further. For instance, Engine Schematics, under the Vehicle Design task, can be decomposed into dozens of subtasks, such as transmission system design and cooling system design.

In our example, the project team for the new vehicle will eventually reach a point at which there is no practical reason to break tasks down further. That point may be when tasks are decomposed into manageable one-week or one-day increments. At that point, work breakdown ends. A WBS typically consists of three to six levels of subdivided activities. The more complex the project, the more levels it will have. As a general rule, stop subdividing tasks when you reach the point at which the work will take an amount of time equal to the smallest time unit you plan to schedule. Thus, if you want to schedule to the nearest day, break down the work to the point at which each task takes a day to perform.

Tips for Doing WBS

Many projects run off track because project team members fail to identify all the tasks and subtasks. Here are a few tips for getting your WBS right:

- Start with the top-most tasks and work downward.

- Involve the people who will have to do the work. They are in the best position to know what is involved with every job and how those jobs can be decomposed into manageable pieces. The project manager and appropriate team members should analyze every task to determine whether all are necessary and whether some can be redesigned to make them faster and less costly to complete.

- Check your work by looking at all the subtasks and seeing whether they add up to the highest-level tasks. Remember, you don't want to miss anything.

Time and Resource Estimates

Once the project manager is satisfied with the breakdown of tasks, a new set of questions must be answered:

- How much time will it take to complete each task?

- What will be the likely cost of completing each task?

- What skills will be needed to complete each task well?

About Time

Let's address the time question first. If the task is familiar—that is, it's something that employees have done many times before—estimating completion time is not difficult. Unfamiliar tasks, in contrast, require much more thinking and discussion. Just remember that these time estimates will eventually be rolled up into a schedule for the entire project, so you want to be as realistic as possible. Grossly underestimating the time component will come back to haunt you later. Here are a few tips for making these time estimates:

- Estimates should be based on experience, using the average expected time to perform a task. The more familiar you or other employees are with a particular task, the more accurate your estimate will be.

- Always remember that estimates are just that—estimates. They're not guarantees, so don't change them into firm commitments at this phase.

- When presenting estimates to stakeholders, make sure that they are aware of all the assumptions and variables built into those calculations. Consider presenting time factors as ranges instead of fixed estimates. For example, say, "Task A will take eight to twelve hours to complete." Any estimate is bound to be wrong; a range, on the other hand, is more likely to be right, because it accounts for natural variations.

- Padding estimates is an acceptable way of reducing the risk of a task (or the entire project) taking longer than the schedule allows. But this practice should be done openly and with full awareness of what you're doing.

About Costs and Skills

Once the time issues have been addressed, the project manager should revisit each task with the goal of determining how much each will cost to complete, what resources will be required, and what specific skills will be necessary. The output of this piece of analysis will indicate the level of financial and resource commitments the organization will have to make. It will also give the manager a much better idea of who, based on needed skills, will be needed on the project team. If the skills are not available within the organization, skill gaps will have to be filled by means of training, hiring people with the requisite skills, and/or contracting with independent specialists—all of which should be factored into the project's cost.

Assigning the Work

With the WBS output in hand, the project manager is now in a position to assign the work. Every task should have an identified owner—someone, not a department, who's responsible for the work. And that owner should have enough time in his or her schedule to complete the assignment.

If the team has not yet been assembled, the project manager should use what is now known about skill requirements to recruit the right people from inside or outside the company. If the team has already been assembled, or if outside recruiting is not allowed, the project manager must do the best he can with the available talent. That means assessing people's skills and matching them as best possible to the task list, using training to fill in skill gaps. If you have worked with the team members before and know their individual strengths well enough, make the assignments yourself. If the team has been assigned and you are unfamiliar with their individual capabilities, create two lists: one with the names of all the people assigned to the project team, and another with all the skills required to successfully complete the work. At your next meeting, go through these lists. Encourage people to talk about their own skills, and give the group responsibility for initially assigning people to the listed tasks. Determining assignments in a group setting allows people to know what everyone else's skills are; it also ensures not only that the right person is assigned to the task, but also that the team members become aware of the finite resources they have available.

If the members cannot think of anyone qualified to handle certain tasks, you'll have to think about training or recruiting. If they assign an individual to a great number of tasks, be certain that this person has the time to do all of that work. Overloading a team member is analogous to creating a plan that relies on a particular machine to operate thirty hours per day! It simply won't work. But it happens. It's common for companies to discover that their projects require one or more people to work all the time. Some actually require a person to be working in two different geographic locations at the same time!

Also check to see whether any team members are not being asked to do enough. Everyone needs to contribute.

An Extended Example

Now that the basic concepts for the work breakdown structure have been described, let's see how one company put it to use in a project named Project Phoenix, whose goal was to install three Web servers and move key databases to a new data center. This case illustrates one approach to specifying tasks and related subtasks and the assignment of time estimates to each. For the sake of simplicity, cost and skill requirements have not been included.

Table 5-1 indicates the major tasks of the project and how each was broken down and described in greater detail. As shown, every major task is specified as one or more Level 1 subtasks, and most are further specified as Level 2 subtasks. Each subtask is assigned an estimated time duration, the total of which is 22 days. This does not mean that the total time needed to complete the project is 22 days, since some tasks can be completed in parallel. For instance, a team member could alert the data center about the arrival of new equipment at the same time that another completes a purchase order and sends it to the equipment vendor.

Note: Appendix A at the end of this book contains a work breakdown structure worksheet like the one shown in table 5-1. You can use it to specify the many tasks in your project.

TABLE 5-1

Project Phoenix Work Breakdown Structure

Major Task	Level 1 Subtasks	Level 2 Subtasks	Level 2 Subtask Duration (days)
Obtain equipment	Purchase 3 servers and 2 databases with equipment to be shipped to new data center	Cut purchase order and submit to vendor	5
		Alert data center that equipment is slated for arrival	2
Prepare and implement equipment	Physically install hardware		2
	Load operating system		1
	Load applications	Load software, including server software, database applications, and required dependencies	2
	Mirror content to new servers	Copy configurations, transfer files to new servers, and load appropriately	3
Test equipment	Ensure connectivity in the network; check database access, functionality		1
Go live	Cut over to new data center	Switch Web and database access to new sites	1
		Run predetermined tests to ensure data accuracy	1
		Check data and content integrity	1
Test again	Let sites burn in for 24 hours and check integrity again		1
Decommission old equipment	Remove old equipment from site	Uninstall equipment; erase software and content	1
		Ship equipment back to inventory	1
		Total Duration (days)	22

Shall We Proceed?

Completion of the work breakdown structure is an important milestone in the project planning process. The outcome of WBS is a rough estimate of how much time will be required to complete the project. The cost and skills that are necessary for completion can be estimated from the same analysis. Taken together, these calculations represent important information that was not available to decision makers and key stakeholders when they first commissioned the project. Thus, they should ask themselves if they really want to proceed:

- Can we afford the project?

- If the project succeeds, will it be worth the cost?

- Do we have the skills needed to succeed?

- Will the project finish in time to make a difference for our business?

Since the organization's investment in the project will be relatively small at this point, those questions are very appropriate, and abandoning the project for any of those reasons would not be terribly painful.

Abandonment, of course, is not the only option if time, money, and skills are insufficient. The other option is to alter the scope of the project itself. If there is insufficient time to hit an important target date, such as a major trade show, or if the project is too costly, you should think about reducing its objectives. Producing part of the project may be better than producing nothing at all. If the requisite skills are not available, think about delaying the project launch until a time when training or recruiting can provide them.

Does your company take a second look at its project plans at this point? It should. Are company executives flexible with respect to project objectives when sufficient time or other resources are lacking? They should be.

Summing Up

- Work breakdown structure (WBS) is a technique used to decompose high-level project goals into the many tasks required to achieve them.

- Once WBS is complete, managers can estimate the time and cost required to complete each task. They can also assign people to the tasks they've identified.

- Stop breaking down task into subtasks when you reach the point at which the work will take an amount of time equal to the smallest time unit you want to schedule. That might be one day or one week.

- Your WBS exercise may reveal some challenging conclusions: The project will cost more than it's worth, the organization lacks the skills to do the job, or the project will take too long to complete. These revelations should make management think twice about proceeding.

Scheduling the Work

Put the Horse Before the Cart

Key Topics Covered in This Chapter

- *The steps of the scheduling process*

- *Checking for bottlenecks*

- *Using Gantt and PERT charts*

- *The critical path*

SCHEDULES MATTER. Project managers use them as mechanisms to sequence and control activities. Executives use them as measures against which to appraise performance. Without them, projects might linger for month after month, consuming resources and missing opportunities.

This chapter introduces a practical process you can follow in creating a workable and realistic schedule for your project. That process has four steps:

1. Identify and define tasks and subtasks through the work breakdown structure method.

2. Examine the relationships between tasks.

3. Create a draft schedule.

4. Optimize the schedule.

Since we've already covered the first step, let's examine each of the others.

Examine the Relationships Between Tasks

Many tasks are related in some way and, as a result, must be performed in a particular sequence. Consider how you normally go about enjoying a cold bottle of beer on a hot summer day. Three tasks are usually involved: (1) opening the bottle, (2) pouring the beer from the bottle into a glass, and (3) consuming the brew. Ahh! There is a dependent relationship between these three activities. Obviously we cannot do Step 2 before we've completed Step 1, and we cannot perform Step 3 until 1 and 2 have been completed. If time is an issue, we could eliminate Step 2 altogether, drinking directly from the bottle. But Step 1 would continue to be an antecedent to Step 3.

Many workplace activities are similarly dependent on other activities. Remember the vehicle project we introduced—the one where ABC Auto Company plans to introduce a new passenger car? That project team must both design and test its new vehicle. But before the project team can test the car, it must build and test both external and internal components. Figure 6-1 maps the necessary relationship between these activities. Here, the project must (1) design the vehicle, (2) build and test both external and internal components, and (3) test the vehicle built from those components. Because of dependencies, these tasks must be scheduled in a linear manner. However, note in the figure that component building and testing can follow two parallel tracks simultaneously—one for external components and another for internal components. Why? Because each of the build-and-test sets of activities is dependent on vehicle design, and not on one another. Recognizing opportunities to work different activities in parallel, as in this example, is one of the ways that managers can reduce the overall time of their projects.

FIGURE 6-1

Task Relationships

**Project network diagram
(Sample automobile project)**

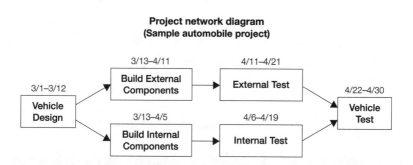

Source: Harvard ManageMentor® on Project Management (Boston: Harvard Business School Publishing, 2002). Used with permission.

Different Dependencies

In some cases, tasks logically have a linear, *finish-to-start* relationship. One task must be finished before another can start, as described below.

Other tasks have a *lagging* relationship. Here, one task must await the start and partial completion of another, as shown below. For an example of a lagging relationship between tasks, consider the development of a new computer system. The software developers must wait until some, but not all, of the hardware development is done. After that point, much of their work can be done in parallel.

```
┌─────────────────────────┐
│  Hardware development    │
└──┬──────────────────────┘
   │   ┌──────────────────────────┐
   └───│  Software development     │
       └──────────────────────────┘
```

Once a project team has evaluated the relationships between tasks, it can diagram them on a whiteboard or, better still, label Post-it notes with the names of discrete tasks and arrange them in the correct order on a large wall. The Post-it note approach is the better choice because changes are easy to make. After some brainstorming and moving of notes from here to there, the project team will eventually be satisfied with its arrangement of dependencies.

Create a Draft Schedule

At this point, the project manager and team have all the information they need to create a draft schedule: a list of tasks, an estimate of the duration of each task, and knowledge of task relationships. We use the term *draft* here because the schedule will have to be fine-tuned once everyone has had a chance to review it, check for bottlenecks, and so forth. The schedule itself should

- indicate start and completion dates for all activities,

- recognize all task duration estimates, and

- recognize task relationships.

Gantt Charts

Many project managers use a Gantt chart for scheduling work. Figure 6-2 represents a Gantt chart for the Phoenix Project introduced earlier. Recall that the project's goal was to install new servers and to get them up and running in a new data center. As you can see, the Phoenix Gantt chart is essentially a bar chart with the tasks listed in the left-hand column and fitted into appropriate time blocks. These blocks indicate when a task should begin, based on task relationships, and when they should end. This type of a diagram can be created using an electronic spreadsheet or a project management software program, such as Microsoft Project. Schedulers can use different colors to indicate which team members are responsible for each block.

Gantt charts show the following:

- Project status (by shading out tasks already completed)

- Estimated project duration

- Estimated task duration

- Task sequences

The popularity of the Gantt chart stems from its simplicity and from its ability to show people the big picture in a single glance. What the Gantt chart does not indicate are the relationships between various tasks. So schedulers must be extra careful to reflect those relationships in the time blocks as they enter the items.

FIGURE 6-2

Gantt Chart

Task or activities	4/8–4/14	4/15–4/21	4/22–4/28	4/29–5/5	5/6–5/12	5/13–5/19	5/20–5/26
Install new servers	███						
Obtain equipment		███					
Implement equipment		███					
Test equipment			███				
Go live with new equipment				███	███	███	
Repeat testing				███	███	███	
Decommission old equipment						███	
Evaluate process							███

Source: Harvard ManageMentor® on Project Management (Boston: Harvard Business School Publishing, 2002), 26. Used with permission.

The Critical Path

Another important piece of information not shown in the Gantt chart is the *critical path*. The critical path is the set of tasks that determines total project duration. It is the longest path through the project, and any delays along it will delay completion of the entire project. In this sense, there is zero slack time within the critical path. While some tasks can be sequenced with much flexibility, critical path tasks are locked in by task relationships.

To identify the critical path, let's revisit the ABC Auto Company project. As described in figure 6-1, the project team broke the Vehicle Design task into various build-and-test subtasks. Take another look at figure 6-1. This graphic is called a *network diagram*. Unlike a Gantt chart, it reveals all the dependent relationships between tasks. It also reveals the critical path, which in this case is (1) Vehicle Design, (2) Build External Components, (3) External Test, and (4) Vehicle Test. Why does this progression of tasks define the critical path? The reason is that it describes the longest path in the diagram. The other path in the diagram, which passes through the Build Internal Components and Internal Test tasks, is shorter by two days. Team members working on those activities could spend two days beyond the number of days budgeted for them and still not affect the scheduled completion of Vehicle Test. Nor would the total project schedule be shortened if members completed their work on non-critical path activities ahead of time. The reason? Tasks on the critical path determine total project duration.

PERT Charts

Some project managers use PERT as an alternative to the Gantt method for scheduling. PERT stands for Performance Evaluation and Review Technique. Figure 6-3 is the PERT chart for the Project Phoenix server installation project described in the Gantt chart (figure 6-2). Each task in the PERT chart is represented by a node that connects with other nodes, or tasks, required to complete the project. A PERT chart may have many parallel or interconnecting

networks of tasks so that periodic reviews are encouraged for complex projects. Unlike the Gantt chart, it indicates all the important
task relationships and project milestones. (Note: The terms PERT
chart and network diagram are practically synonymous.)

Which scheduling tool is best for your purpose? The best
method is the one with which you are comfortable and that does the
job. Don't be lured into using something just because everyone else
does or because it's the latest thing. Take a hard look at how you like
to work, and use the scheduling method that best fits your habits.

To assess which method might suit you best, look at the system
you use for tracking and scheduling your own work. Are you satisfied with it? If you are, this system may be the way to go with tracking and scheduling the entire project. But remember that a system's
usefulness comes from its ability to inform all the team members of
what is going on and to keep them aware that they are part of a
larger effort.

FIGURE 6-3

Project Phoenix PERT Chart

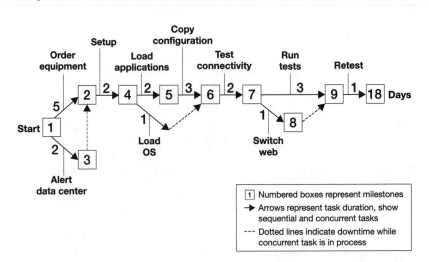

Source: Harvard ManageMentor® on Project Management (Boston: Harvard Business School Publishing, 2002), 25. Used with permission.

Tips for Creating a Draft Project Schedule

- Develop a list of specific tasks.

- Assign a deliverable to each activity—for instance, "prototype for market testing."

- Use deliverables as a basis for creating a project schedule with realistic milestones and due dates.

- Identify bottlenecks that add time to the schedule.

- Determine ways to eliminate bottlenecks, or find ways to work around them.

- Establish a protocol for updating and revising the schedule.

- Keep all stakeholders involved in and informed of the project's progress and all schedule modifications.

Optimize the Schedule

The final step of the scheduling process is optimization. Here, the project manager and team take a very critical look at the draft schedule and seek ways to improve it—that is, to make it more accurate, more realistic, more effective, and faster. Like a writer looking for ways to eliminate unnecessary words from his sentences and add necessary transitions, the project manager should look for the following:

- **Errors**. Are all time estimates realistic? Pay particular attention to time estimates for tasks on the critical path. If any of these tasks cannot be completed on time, the entire schedule will be off. Also, review the relationships between tasks. Does your schedule reflect the fact that some tasks may have to start simultaneously and that others cannot start until some other task is completed or partially completed?

- **Oversights**. Have any tasks or subtasks been left out of the work breakdown structure? Has time for training and maintenance been overlooked in the schedule?

- **Overcommitments**. A review may find that some employees would have to work ten to twelve hours per day for months on end to complete the tasks assigned to them in the schedule. Likewise, a piece of equipment may be booked in the schedule for output in excess of its known capacity. If you find these overcommitments, distribute part of the load to others.

- **Bottlenecks**. A bottleneck is any task that causes the work feeding it to pile up. Think of an auto assembly line that has to stop periodically because the people who install the seats cannot keep up with the pace of the line. The usual way to handle this is (a) to improve the work process used in that task (that is, to speed it up) or (b) to shift resources into that task—for example, by adding more people or better machinery.

- **Imbalances in the workload**. A schedule review may indicate that some team members are being asked to carry more than their share of the load while others are being asked to do very little. Balancing the load could reduce the overall schedule.

- **Opportunities to reduce the schedule**. Because tasks on the critical path define the duration of the entire project, look very carefully at them. You may be able to shorten them by shifting more of your resources to them, as in the bottleneck problem. It may be possible to take these resources from noncritical path tasks. For example, if you have four people working on a task that has four to five days of slack time, shift some or all of those people onto a critical path task for several days.

Using Scheduling Software

A number of software packages are available to help you develop and manage your schedule. To figure out which software is best for you, get recommendations from users. Then check their work habits against your own to see whether the software is a good fit. Unless you are already familiar with the software, build time into your personal schedule to learn it. Mastery may require that you can get reliable training and technical support for the program.

Software is a wonderful tool when you know how to make the most of it. It can keep track of times and tasks; produce clear, eye-catching schedule charts; and so forth. It is helpful but not infallible. It won't check for faulty time estimates or dependencies you may have overlooked in putting together the schedule. So review every task in the schedule carefully with another team member or stakeholder before entering it into the software.

Any project planning software you plan to use should do the following:

- Handle development of and changes to Gantt charts and network diagrams, including PERT charts and calculations of critical paths

- Provide on-screen previews of information before printing

- Produce schedules and budgets

- Integrate project schedules with a calendar allowing for weekends and holidays

- Create different scenarios for contingency planning and updating

- Check for overscheduling of individuals and groups

Summing Up

- Once all the tasks and subtasks have been identified, examine the relationships between tasks to see which must follow a particular sequence and which can be worked in parallel.

- A draft schedule includes the start and completion dates of all activities, recognizes task durations, and illustrates the dependencies between tasks.

- Gantt charts provide a useful visualization of project status, estimated project and task duration, and task sequences, but they do not reflect underlying task dependencies or the critical path.

- The critical path is the longest path through a project. It represents the total project duration.

- Any delay along the critical path will derail the entire project.

- PERT charts and network diagrams serve the same purposes as the Gantt chart but also indicate the critical path and all important task dependencies.

7

Adjustments and Trade–Offs

More Fine Tuning

Key Topics Covered in This Chapter

- *What to do when a project cannot meet all the expectations of the sponsor and other stakeholders*

- *Challenging assumptions, deadlines, resource allocations, and stated deliverables*

- *Reevaluating the schedule, its underlying tasks, and task assignments*

WE'VE ALREADY EXPLORED how a complex project can be broken down into a manageable set of component tasks and how those tasks can be scheduled. These two key project activities are likely to uncover discrepancies between the objectives stated in the charter and what the project team can deliver—and when. The work breakdown schedule exercise, for example, may reveal that company personnel are incapable of completing certain tasks. Likewise, scheduling may indicate that the project cannot be finished within the time frame anticipated by key stakeholders. Faced with these discrepancies, the project manager, sponsor, and team members must make adjustments and trade-offs. This chapter discusses a number of options for getting a project to fit with constraints like time and skills.

When the Project Won't Fit

Some projects cannot be realistically completed within the time frame or budget initially conceived by sponsors and key stakeholders. Work breakdown structure and scheduling bring these problems to the surface. Project managers should confront them head-on by bringing them to the attention of the sponsor and key stakeholders. Consider this example:

> *Antonia and her project team have just completed the final, optimizing step of the scheduling process. They reviewed their work breakdown structure, adding several subtasks that someone had overlooked in the*

draft schedule. They reassessed the time anticipated for each task, with particular attention to those on the critical path. And they did whatever they could to redeploy resources to make the schedule as short and as realistic as possible. But they couldn't get the schedule to conform to their sponsor's expected completion date.

"We have a big problem," Antonia told her team. "We must have a working preproduction model of the new implantable cell phone in time for the big MicroCom trade show, which opens in Houston exactly forty weeks from today. But the current schedule will make us almost a month late. Harold isn't going to like this, and Carla will go ballistic."

Harold was the company's vice president of technology and sponsor of the development project; Carla was the vice president of marketing. Antonia recalled her last meeting with Carla. "This is a huge opportunity for us," Carla had told her. "Can you image how upscale people will respond to the possibility of taking calls anywhere at any time without using a phone set, and without anyone hearing their ringing phone? With a coin-sized receiver/transmitter implanted under their collarbone, they'll be able to listen and talk hands-free while walking down the street, swimming laps in the pool, or sitting in a movie theater."

Antonia would have to tell Carla and Harold that her project team would not be able to develop and test a working model of the implantable phone in time for the all-important trade show. What else could she do?

Antonia's situation is not uncommon. Project ideas emerge from many sources: brainstorming sessions by senior managers, serendipitous discoveries in the laboratory, the emergence of a market threat, and so forth. Each of these sources produces a request for action. The executives who sponsor projects are, if nothing else, action oriented by experience. They give orders and expect their subordinates to follow through. The careful planning that follows (work breakdown structure and scheduling), however, is bound to uncover contradictions that action-oriented executives may have overlooked. What sponsors and other key stakeholders expect cannot always be achieved under their initial terms—despite the efforts of project team members to make it happen.

What can be done under these circumstances? In the example just described, what should Antonia say to Harold, the sponsor, and to Carla, a key stakeholder?

Challenge Assumptions

Most projects are formed on a foundation of assumptions. There is $1 million available to complete the project—and no more. The number of people on the project must be limited to twenty-five. The project must be completed by March 30 of next year. The new product must be no larger than 15 cm. by 10 cm. by 4 cm.

Where do these figures and specifications come from? Some may come off the top of someone's head without a great deal of thought—not the product of careful reflection, measurement, or calculation. Certainly, neither the sponsor nor any of the key shareholders produced these figures through the careful work breakdown structure and scheduling exercises demonstrated earlier. Let's reflect on some of these key assumptions.

The Deadline

Consider Carla's drop-dead date for a working model of the implantable cell phone. Per Carla, it *must* be available in time for the big Houston trade show. But if that didn't happen, would this innovative new product fail or its commercial prospects diminish? Would key customers who heard of the new device two months after the Houston trade show or who saw it demonstrated via Web-cast be less receptive? Is the MicroCom tradeshow the *only* way to introduce this product to the public? Those questions must be answered. There is a possibility that Carla's assumption is untested or wrong.

Available Resources

A project's charter should state the resources available for the work. But faced with a problem like Antonia's, and the importance of the outcome, the project manager, sponsor, and stakeholders should discuss the possibility of supplementing the originally allotted personnel, funding, and so forth. Giving the project more resources might bring the schedule in line with stakeholder requirements. For example, if Carla's sales and marketing people absolutely must have the new device available at the trade show, then these tactics might be considered:

- Assign more employees to the project, particularly to tasks on the critical path.

- Outsource one or more tasks to qualified vendors or suppliers.

- Buy, instead of build, components whose development will add time to the schedule.

Decision makers are faced with a trade-off here: Shift resources from one organizational activity to another. They must consider the situation and determine whether exchanging one value for another will produce a better overall outcome.

Facing up to trade-offs is one of the most common and important challenges of project management—one that many managers fail to master. Too often stakeholders like Carla and sponsors like Harold demand that their impossible requirements be met and are disappointed when project managers fail to deliver. When project managers tell them, "Given the available time and resources, I can do X or Y. Which do you want?" The stakeholders reply, "Both." When the project manager cannot do that, he or she takes the blame.

The best antidote to this problem is a process that makes necessary trade-offs visible and that involves stakeholders in their resolution. Indeed, stakeholders *must* take responsibility for these trade-offs.

Project Deliverables

The third area in which a scheduling solution might be sought involves the deliverables stated in the project charter. Those deliverables might be a finished product (for example, a bridge ready to receive vehicle traffic), a plan ready for implementation (for example, a complete marketing plan for the coming calendar year), or, as in the implantable cell phone case, a working prototype. Whatever the deliverable happens to be, its specifications may be negotiable to some degree, especially if the sponsor and key stakeholders cannot or will not relax the deadline or contribute more resources to the cause.

Whether and how specifications can be altered is, of course, determined entirely by the situation. In the cell phone case, Antonia spoke with Harold and Carla about their requirements for the working preproduction model that Carla insists must be ready in forty weeks.

> *"My team has revisited the schedule," said Antonia, "and we believe that we can have the implantable cell phone ready for the Houston trade show. However, to do that, we will have to relax one of the specifications given to us in the charter."*
>
> *"Which one is that?" Harold asked.*
>
> *"The switching capabilities of the microprocessor," she replied. "We could reduce the end-to-end project schedule by five weeks if you'd be willing to use a working model that could handle only the most basic cell phone features—that is, a model that could not use the call-waiting, voice mail, and caller identification features planned for the final product. That concession would allow us to meet your trade show deadline. We'd save that time by adapting an existing microprocessor."*
>
> *"Would that serve your purposes?" Harold asked Carla.*
>
> *"Well, it's not ideal," she replied. "We wouldn't be able to demonstrate the full range of product features in Houston."*
>
> *"That's true," Harold interjected, "but the thing that will get people's attention—and create a buzz—will be the ability to receive a call by simply touching one's collarbone and talking hands-free. That's the real breakthrough in this product. It's unlikely that anyone will even ask about those other features."*
>
> *"You're probably right," Carla conceded. "We could indicate that the other features will be included in the first release model."*
>
> *"Good," said Antonia. "If you can live with that as a deliverable, we can meet your schedule."*

The discussions that project managers, key stakeholders, and sponsors have around the issues just described require that people are willing and able to set priorities. Is the delivery date the highest priority? Is it secondary to the original set of deliverables? If more resources are needed to make the project work, from which other activities should they be taken? Those are questions with which decision makers must grapple.

Revisit Tasks and Times

There is a good chance that challenging assumptions about the project's deadline, available resources, and deliverables will uncover opportunities to adapt the project to the schedule. In some cases, it may be necessary to relax more than one of those constraints to obtain the right fit. But there is also a chance that none of those solutions will help—in which case the project team must revisit its earlier work. That means:

- **Reevaluate the work breakdown structure (WBS)**. Is every one of the tasks and subtasks listed in the WBS necessary? Get rid of any that are not, as long as their deletion will not imperil the project. Are the estimated times needed to complete these tasks realistic, or have some been padded? If any are overstated, make them more realistic.

- **Reevaluate your initial assignment of tasks**. Are the current owners of each task the best possible choices? If not, try to recruit individuals who can do these jobs faster and better. Doing so might ruffle some feathers but may be necessary to get your project finished on schedule. The organizational clout of the sponsor might be instrumental in obtaining the services of these high-performing individuals. Sponsor intervention is necessary when managers resist any attempt to move their best employees away from their regular departmental duties.

- **Redirect resources to get the highest possible performance**. Are any of your best people or other resources tied up in activities that aren't on the critical path? If they are, do some thoughtful shuffling. Then reestimate the time needed to complete the affected tasks. You may find that this reshuffling has improved your schedule.

- **Streamline key tasks**. Business's experience with process reengineering during the 1990s demonstrated something of profound importance: Many tasks could be made faster and better through redesign. Bank loan applications that once took ten days were completed in a few hours without any decrease in quality. Customer orders that once took several days to process and pack were shipped the same day. There may be opportunities to do the same with tasks on your project's critical path. Have you examined those tasks from a redesign perspective?

Theoretically, those practices should go into the final, optimizing step of the project scheduling process. But if that step fails to align the schedule with the charter's requirements and if the sponsor will not allow any adjustments, you'll have to approach the job with greater determination.

Summing Up

- If it's clear that a project cannot produce the deliverables specified by the sponsor or meet the sponsor's deadline, attack the problem head-on through discussion with him or her. Don't ignore the problem.

- Revisit key assumptions about deliverables, deadline requirements, and project resources. It may be possible to satisfy the sponsor and stakeholders by making adjustments to those elements.

- Revisit the work breakdown structure and your initial assignment of tasks to identify unnecessary steps and opportunities to get jobs done faster and better.

8

Managing Risk

Scanning the Hazy Horizon

Key Topics Covered in This Chapter

* *Identifying and prioritizing risks to the project plan*

* *Avoiding and minimizing risks*

* *Contingency planning*

EVERY PROJECT PLAN includes assumptions—about task performance by project team members, the time required to complete key tasks, the future availability of resources, the collaboration of allies, and so forth. Risks lurk in each of these assumptions. What if the techies in the R&D lab cannot produce a workable prototype? What if a key member of the project team is hospitalized for a month—or leaves the company? How would the project be affected if a supplier to whom you have outsourced an important task falls a month behind schedule? Managers deal with risks like these every day:

- **Financial resource risk**. A financial manager, foreseeing a possible cash flow shortage, reduces the risk by collecting receivables ahead of schedule, putting a hold on all discretionary spending, and making sure that a bank credit line is available.

- **Human resource risk**. When informed that a key employee, Jack, has been interviewing with other companies, his boss takes some initial steps in finding a replacement. "Who could fill Jack's shoes tomorrow if need be?" the boss asks himself. "If no one is quite ready, what training or experience would our best internal candidates for the job need to make them ready?"

- **Supply risk**. A purchasing manager for an original equipment manufacturer, fearful that the supply of a key component may be extremely tight six months in the future, reduces the risk by building a buffer stock.

- **Quality risk**. A real estate developer awards contracts to many building contractors. Knowing from past experience that many low-cost bidders will cut corners to finish within budget, the developer builds quality specifications into every contract and monitors compliance on a regular basis.

Each of those managers recognized the risks to their operations and took steps to mitigate those risks. Doing so is part of their jobs. As a project manager or participant, you must do the same.

What Is Risk Management?

Risk management is the part of project planning that identifies key risks and develops plans to prevent them and/or mitigate their adverse effects. In reality there are two types of risk management. Risk management Type 1 assumes a certain amount of clairvoyance—it expects that it is possible to anticipate developments that could compromise the plan or the schedule. Risk management Type 2 recognizes that some adverse developments cannot be anticipated. There can be no contingency planning around this form of risk. The only remedy is to build a robust management framework that's capable of dealing with the unexpected—whatever it might be. This chapter focuses on the first form of risk management; Type 2 risk will be developed more fully later.

Risk management in the traditional, Type 1 sense has three essential aims:

1. Identify and prioritize risks to the project.

2. Take actions to avoid or minimize key risks.

3. Develop contingency plans to handle potential setbacks.

Let's consider each of those activities.

Identify and Prioritize Project Risks

The most obvious way to deal with risk is to conduct a systematic audit of all the things that could go wrong with your project. A risk audit involves the following three steps:

1. **Collect ideas widely**. People's perspectives about risk differ greatly. Some foresee perils that others miss entirely. By talking with many people—project team members, people in the operating units or on the corporate staff, customers, and suppliers— you may harvest some surprising information. For example, a supplier may tell the manager of a product-development project that his rival is working on a product for the same market and that its development appears to be much further along than his. There's a good chance that the rival will beat him to market.

2. **Identify internal risks**. Understaffing can be a source of risk. One key resignation, for example, could cause an important project to collapse. Poorly trained quality assurance personnel represent another source of internal risk. Their substandard work may eventually allow defective or dangerous products to reach customers, resulting in a costly product recall, lawsuits, and a public relations fiasco.

3. **Identify external risks**. An external risk may take the form of an emerging new technology—one that will render your new product line obsolete. An impending regulatory change may be another. External risks are many and often hidden. Some large technology companies maintain small "business intelligence" units to identify these threats.

As you conduct your risk audit, pay particular attention to areas with the greatest potential to harm your project. Depending on the project, these areas might include health and environmental issues, technical breakdowns, economic and market volatility, or relationships with customers and suppliers. Ask yourself where your project is most vulnerable. Then consider these questions: What are the worst things that could go wrong in these areas? Which risks are the most likely to surface?

A Method for Quantifying Risk

Your risk audit will likely identify dozens of risks to your project. Naturally, some will be more dangerous than others—that is, their potential for damage will be greater. At the same time, some risks are more likely to occur than are others. Thus, risk has two factors you must consider: potential negative impact and probability of occurrence. You can use them to prioritize your audit list. Here are four steps for auditing risk:

1. Make an estimate of the negative impact of each risk. Express it in monetary form. For example, "The cost of a one-month delay would be $25,000."

2. Assign a probability to the risk (0 percent to 100 percent). For example, "The risk of a one-month delay is 40 percent."

3. Multiply the monetary impact by the probability. Example: $25,000 x 0.40 = $10,000. Statisticians call this the expected value. In effect, it is the dollar impact weighted by the probability of its occurrence.

4. Rank order your audit list by expected value.

A rank-order list will give you greater insights into the risks you face.

Take Actions to Avoid or Minimize Risks

Once you have audited your situation and identified the key risks, you will be positioned to do something about them. In the most drastic cases, you may alter the project's scope to avoid risks that the organization is not prepared to confront. For example, a sausage maker, fearful of bacterial contamination somewhere in the production or distribution channel, may decide to produce only precooked and aseptically packaged meats. In another case, the project manager may take positive steps to prevent risks from emerging as full-blown crises. For example, if you are concerned that a key project member,

Brenda, may leave the company, here are a few things you could do to eliminate the risk or minimize its consequences:

- Make sure that Brenda has a visible and attractive career course ahead of her within the company.

- Prepare other employees to fill Brenda's shoes in the event that she leaves.

- Don't give Brenda responsibility for too many important tasks; instead, distribute important tasks among several reliable project team members. Doing so will diversify your risk.

Still other risks identified in your audit can be minimized through thoughtful planning. For example, if customer requirements for some aspect of your project's new product are fast changing, you can minimize the risk through project planning. Consider this case:

Gizmo Ergonomics Company has launched a project to introduce a new, high-priced office chair. The project team is confident that all but one of the customer requirements revealed through intensive research will remain valid two years from now, when the product is introduced to market. That one dubious requirement is color. "One year everyone wants black or gray," complained the project manager, "and the next year maroon is the in color. It's impossible to know in advance which color will appeal to customers."

Color choice is a big risk for this project. Gizmo's people could diversify the risk by producing its new chair in four or five colors, hoping that one or two of them will be popular with customers when the product hits market. But that strategy would create an expensive inventory problem and still not address the entire color risk.

In the end, the project team designed the color risk out of its development plan. Taking a tip from Benetton, the Italian apparel maker, the team designed the product and its manufacturing process in a way that made color selection the final phase of manufacturing. "We will build items to stock without any fabric," said the manufacturing manager. "Once we have an order, we can quickly install the customer's choice of upholstery. In effect, we will carry no finished stock."

Brainstorm the Possibilities

Brainstorming sessions that include many people with different functions and different perspectives is usually the most productive approach to identifying risks and finding ways to minimize their impact. There is real power in numbers since no single person can foresee the dozens of things that could go wrong in a project, especially a large one. As you brainstorm, develop a list of serious risks, and then unify similar ones into manageable groups. Try to identify the underlying basis for those risks. For instance, the basis of risk for the office chair maker is the customer's choice of fabric color. Once you understand the sources of risk, you'll be in a better position to steer clear of them.

Develop Contingency Plans to Handle Potential Setbacks

Some risks cannot be avoided. Others can be reduced, but only in part. Contingency plans should be developed for these unavoidable and uncontrollable risks. A *contingency plan* is a course of action prepared in advance to deal with a potential problem; it answers this question: "If _____ happens, how could we respond in a way that would neutralize or minimize the damage?" Here are two examples of project contingency plans:

- The Acme Company set up a two-year project to modernize its manufacturing facilities. Senior management regarded the two-year deadline as extremely important. Recognizing the real risk that the deadline might not be met, the sponsor agreed to set up a reserve fund that could be used to hire outside help if the project fell behind schedule. This contingency plan included a monthly progress review and a provision that falling three or more weeks behind schedule would trigger release of the reserve funds. In addition, two managers were charged with the job of identifying no less than three vendors who were capable of helping with the project.

- TechoWhiz, Inc. was banking on its software project team to develop a new version of its integrated business application suite, one that would include all the bells and whistles, and seamless linkages to the Internet. Not wanting to miss the announced release date and expensive marketing rollout, the team developed a contingency plan for dealing with any unfinished elements of the program—and the probability of having some was high. That contingency plan was straightforward: Any feature not ready at the time of the official release would be offered at a future date to all registered users of the new version as a downloadable add-on. Staffing for development of add-on elements was planned in advance, with budgeting contingent on the amount of needed work.

The real benefit of a contingency plan is that it prepares the project and its company to deal quickly and effectively with adverse situations. When disaster strikes, managers and project members with such a plan can act immediately; they don't have to spend weeks trying to figure out what they should do or how they will find the funds to deal with their new situation. The what and how of their response will be contained in the plan.

Has your project identified its risks? Does it know which have the greatest expected value? Has it developed contingency plans for dealing with them?

Make Someone Responsible for Each Serious Risk and Its Management

Just as every task on the project's schedule should have an owner, every key risk should be someone's responsibility. That person should monitor the assigned risk, sound the alarm if it appears to be moving from potential problem to real problem, and take charge of the consequences.

Summing Up

- Risk management identifies key risks and develops plans to prevent them and/or mitigate their adverse effects.

- A risk audit identifies things that could wrong.

- Brainstorming sessions that involve many people with different functions and perspectives are usually the best way to conduct a risk audit.

- Develop contingency plans for important risks that cannot be avoided or greatly reduced.

9

Project Adaptation

Dealing with What You Cannot Anticipate

Key Topics Covered in This Chapter

- *Three sources of unanticipated project risk*

- *How management inflexibility on budgets and deadlines has led to disastrous surprises*

- *A model for adaptive project management— and when to apply it*

I N   W A R F A R E , initial battle plans begin falling apart with the first skirmishes. Combatants are forced to respond to moves that were not—or could not—have been anticipated. Challenges and opportunities reveal themselves as events play out. Big, complex projects—even those that are well planned—experience something very similar. Customer requirements change even as the project team is working to satisfy them; the team discovers that it is aiming at a moving target. Unforeseen opportunities to do something of greater value for customers are encountered in the course of executing the existing project plan. Project prototypes lead to dead ends or reveal the need for more development. One of the key consultants working with the team is pulled away for a month to serve another client. Project participants are learning about a new technology and its capabilities even as they attempt to install it.

Each of those examples is a development that may not have been anticipated, no matter how smart or prepared project participants were in the beginning. Earlier we explained a traditional form of risk management; it included risks that can be anticipated and addressed through avoidance and contingency plans. Here we are concerned with risks that are less likely to be anticipated. In prototyping, for example, it is difficult to understand the risks and possibilities until you've actually tried something. Consider a major information-technology installation. Here, the project team is dealing with new and unfamiliar technology that it has not yet mastered. And because the technology is new, customers are not in a good position to articulate the deliverables they expect from the project. The project's unfolding is punctuated by dead ends, disappointments, and valuable discoveries.

The traditional framework of project management has not been particularly useful in dealing with hard-to-anticipate risks. The tools offered in earlier chapters—work breakdown structure, time estimates, and scheduling methods—definitely help, especially when project personnel are familiar with the tasks and technologies with which they must engage, and when outcomes are highly measurable. As author and Harvard Business School professor Robert Austin has stated: "Conventional project management methodologies work best when the chances are really good that the project will unfold as anticipated during its planning stages, when there is little that can happen during the project that planners can't see coming, when you can formulate responses to contingencies in advance. In other words: when there is not much genuine discovery going on."[1] He points to building construction as an example, where the range of potential problems often can be anticipated and solutions planned in advance. The traditional tools of project management, however, are less useful when uncertainty is high. Something more is required: adaptability.

This chapter provides practical advice for dealing with hard-to-anticipate risk—that is, it explains how you can (and should) be prepared to adapt and learn as a project unfolds and as participants make discoveries and encounter unanticipated problems and opportunities.

Sources of Unanticipated Risk— and Their Consequences

The risks that project managers cannot anticipate generally come from three sources:

1. New and unfamiliar technology (for example, development and installation of totally new enterprise software)

2. Work that is outside the experience of the project planner and project team (for example, a team of auto-body designers accustomed to working with sheet metal attempts to switch to high-impact plastic)

3. Project magnitude (for example, a team of architects and building contractors who have never built anything higher than a
   four-story building tackle a fifty-story office structure)

The consequences of the risks in those sources are largely felt in the
implementation phase of projects. Those consequences can be huge
in terms of project cost, schedule slippage, and disappointing results.
Managers of Boston's infamous Big Dig highway project, for example, were forced to reveal in 2001 that the venture was several *billion*
dollars over budget and a year or more behind schedule. In another
example, a major financial services company reported receiving no
benefit from hundreds of millions of dollars invested in a new IT system; the project was a total loss.

The Perils of IT Projects

Because of their reliance on new technology and their organization-wide scope, information-technology projects are particularly susceptible to unanticipated risk. Anecdotal evidence
suggests that more than 50 percent are outright failures. In describing their perils, three Harvard Business School professors
put it this way:

*Despite 40 years of accumulated experience in managing informa-
tion technology (IT) projects, the day of the big disaster on a major
IT project has not passed. Why? An analysis of these examples
and a preponderance of research over the last 10 years suggest three
serious deficiencies. . . : (1) failure to assess the implementation risk
of a project at the time it is funded; (2) failure to consider the ag-
gregate implementation risk of a portfolio of projects; and (3) failure to recognize that different projects require different managerial
approaches.*[a]

[a] Lynda M. Applegate, Robert D. Austin, and F. Warren McFarlan, *Corporate Information Strategy and Management*, 6th ed. (Burr Ridge, IL: McGraw-Hill/Irwin, 2003), 269–270.

Another consequence of applying the traditional project management discipline to situations with high uncertainty—where things are likely to go wrong—is a tendency for participants to be silent about problems. Being on time and on schedule are so important that some people are afraid to come forward with the truth about inevitable problems with budgets, schedules, and technical roadblocks. Admitting to a problem is the equivalent to admitting a personal failure. You can almost hear the sponsor saying, "You agreed at the very beginning that you could get the job done in six months if you had a $300,000 budget and a team of five people. So why isn't the job finished?"

Not surprisingly, many people simply ignore their problems, hoping that a breakthrough or piece of good luck will make things right in the end—which almost never happens. Others hope that problems and their consequences will not be revealed until much later—or that their personal connection with those problems will not be known. For example, software developers may be tempted to take shortcuts because nonspecialist managers are unlikely to trace complex systems problems to their sources.[2] In a case that involved one of the Big Three U.S. automakers, a new, three-year, multibillion-dollar vehicle platform project was under tremendous pressure from higher management to be completed on time. The company's engineers and designers were attempting something they had never done: introducing a compact car that could go head-to-head with those built by Japanese rivals. As the project entered its final months, it was clear to people in the trenches that the new vehicle had major problems, yet no one wanted to acknowledge them. Senior management wouldn't tolerate any bad news. So the new vehicle was pushed on from one development stage to another with all of its defects. For example, when it failed its low temperature start-up test, someone fudged the numbers, giving it a passing grade. When a preproduction model arrived at the company's outdoor track for road testing, engineers altered its carburetor and filled the tank with a special fuel; the car could not make it around the track without that assistance. Management was clueless about the vehicle's problems, which became devastatingly clear once it entered the market.

In a comparable case, this one involving a major U.S. manufacturer, managers for a multimillion-dollar IT implementation project deliberately silenced systems analysts who had discovered substantial technical problems. The systems analysts were saying "This won't work. The plan must change." These were words the project managers didn't want anyone to hear. After all, they had a plan, and the plan had to be implemented. In the end, their failure to heed the analysts' warnings—and to adapt the plan to a new reality—cost the company millions.

The disasters experienced by these companies might have been avoided or mitigated if people had not been so locked into their plans. What happens when projects at your organization encounter serious and unanticipated problems?

The Adaptive Management Approach

Is the object of your project or its implementation shrouded in uncertainty? Is it based on a new technology or new material with which your team is unfamiliar? Are the tasks involved different than anything your team has dealt with in the past? Is the project substantially larger than any others in your experience?

If you answered yes to one or more of those questions, the traditional management tools—work breakdown structure, time estimates, and scheduling methods—might not be optimal. You may have to consider a more adaptive approach.

A traditional model for project management is basically a linear progression of activities: define and organize, plan and schedule the work, manage execution, and close down. (For a graphic representation, see figure 1-1.) Feedback loops provide opportunities for learning to flow back into different components of the model. But, at bottom, this model is linear; one that inherently assumes that project planners know what needs to be done, what it will cost to do it, and how much time it will take. The traditional model is workable for many, if not most, projects, but it's less helpful for those with high levels of uncertainty. But what can be used in those exceptional cases?

In their research of large IT implementation projects, Lynda Applegate, Robert Austin, and Warren McFarlan found that some companies—notably Cisco Systems and Tektronix—have enjoyed success with adaptive project management models that do the following:[3]

1. **Approach tasks iteratively**. Members are engaged in small incremental tasks. The outcomes of those tasks are evaluated and adjustments are made moving forward.

2. **Have fast cycles**. Long lead times interfere with the iterative approach.

3. **Emphasize early value delivery**. Instead of delivering value at project end, deliverables come earlier and in smaller pieces. This encourages feedback and the incorporation of learning into subsequent activities.

4. **Staff the project with people who are capable of learning and adapting**. Some people are faster learners than others and are more amenable to change.

5. **Put less reliance on decision-making tools that assume predictability**. Return on investment, net present value, and internal rate of return are useful decision tools, but only when future cash flows are reasonably predictable—which is not the case in projects with high uncertainty.

Cisco refers to its project approach as "rapid iterative prototyping." Here, many tasks are viewed as probes—as learning experiences for subsequent steps. This tactic is analogous to the notion of the "cheap kills" that research and development personnel use to sort through many possibilities quickly and at low cost. When the right solution is not apparent, they try a number of simple experiments to separate promising and unpromising options. Even failed experiments provide insights into what will work. This experimental, adaptive approach to project management depends on a project team that is curious, open to learning, and eager to cycle its learning into each new step.

Rapid Iterative Prototyping— Nineteenth-Century Style

Thomas A. Edison, America's innovation icon, never used the expressions "cheap kills" as far as we know. And he certainly never heard the term "rapid iterative prototyping." He did, however, practice both.

In 1878, Edison jumped into the race to develop the first practical incandescent lamp. Many others were already in the field, but he reasoned that he stood a chance to win.

Edison knew—as did his competitors—that passing an electrical current through a wire or other conductive filament would make it glow brightly. He also knew that higher voltage would make the filament glow more brightly, but that it would also cause the filament to burn up more quickly. One of the key challenges, then, was to find a filament material that would glow brightly without quickly burning up.

What material should he try? No amount of advanced planning could have answered that essential question. So Edison and his "Insomnia Brigade" of assistants (so-called because of their boss's demanding work hours) set out on a course of cheap kills. They tested thousands of filaments in a vacuum—filaments made from chromium, aluminum, papers coiled in various ways, and other materials. They eventually found a material that worked well—a piece of carbonized cotton thread.

Edison beat his many competitors to the patent office, and his practice of making cheap kills, or rapid iterative prototyping if you will, made it possible.

SOURCE: Adapted with permission from James M. Utterback, *Mastering the Dynamics of Innovation* (Boston: Harvard Business School Publishing, 1994), 58–62.

The adaptive approach points to a new role for project sponsors. In the traditional model, the sponsor says, "Here's what I want. To get it, I will provide your project with a budget of $2 million and eighteen people." Writing in *Science*'s Next Wave, Robert Austin suggests a different approach, one that conforms more closely to the approach used by venture capitalists (VCs). Venture capitalists, he notes, seldom give entrepreneurs a big pile of cash at the beginning of their work. Instead, VCs stage their commitment as their entrepreneurial partners produce results.[4] For example, if the entrepreneur has a start-up software company with a plan to develop a breakthrough application, the VC will provide only enough cash for the project to move forward to the next level. If the entrepreneur succeeds in reaching that level, the VC will review progress and develop expectations for the next step. Here, the results of the just-completed step provide new information for the VC, who will finance the following step if the prospects are favorable.

The venture capitalist advances cash to probe and seek feedback—that is, to purchase information, learn, and reduce uncertainty. Each investment gives him an option to remain in the game—if there is a game! In effect, the financier pays to preserve his option to do more.

In this adaptive model, key project activities move forward through a series of learning experiences as represented graphically in figure 9-1.

FIGURE 9-1

The Adaptive Model of Project Management

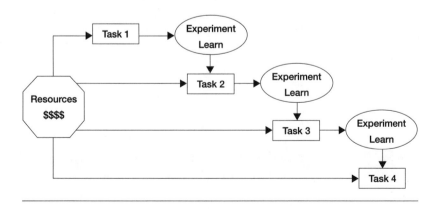

The adaptive model does not apply to every project, but it's recommended when the level of planning or execution uncertainty is high—that is, when the project faces risks that may not be anticipated, or when the range of potential outcomes is very wide. How uncertain is your current project? Is your company ready for this adaptive approach? Are you?

Summing Up

- The traditional project model is not particularly adaptive when the level of unanticipated risk is high.

- Unanticipated risks generally have three main sources: new and unfamiliar technology; a new kind of work; and a project magnitude that is substantially larger than those with which the team has experience.

- Insistence on strict adherence to budgets and deadlines can be dangerous when uncertainty is high; it can make people ignore or conceal problems.

- The adaptive project management model encourages people to do the following: to engage in small incremental tasks, to evaluate their outcomes and make adjustments, to avoid long lead times, to emphasize early value delivery, to staff projects with skilled people who are capable of learning and adapting, and to put less reliance on decision tools that assume predictability.

10

Getting Off on
the Right Foot

Project Needs to Keep in Mind

Key Topics Covered in This Chapter

- *The importance of the project launch meeting, and what should be addressed*

- *Integrative mechanisms that encourage collaboration and bonds of trust between project team members*

- *Norms of team behavior*

PROJECTS that get off on the right foot have a greater likelihood of success. Project planning, a formal charter, work structure breakdown, careful scheduling, and risk management are part of that process. But there's more, and it's covered here.

Once a team has been formed, the charter delivered, and the work scheduled, several important things must be done before work commences. First, the project needs a launch—a special event that marks the official beginning of the project's work. Second, the project manager must attend to a number of important issues associated with team-based work. At bottom, project management is very much about leading teams. Indeed, team-based work is at the heart of every project. Finally, the norms of behavior that make collaborative, team-based work possible must be instituted and communicated to all participants.

Why Launch Meetings Matter

An official project launch represents the very first project milestone, telling everyone, "We begin this journey together, and we begin now." If conducted properly, the launch has substantial symbolic value.

The best way to launch a project effort is through an all-team meeting, one with appropriate levels of gravity and fanfare. Much discussion and planning will obviously have been undertaken prior to the launch meeting, involving the project manager, the sponsor, and key individual members. But those informal get-togethers are no substitute for a face-to-face meeting attended by all members, the sponsor, key stakeholders, and, if appropriate, the highest-ranking official of the organization.

Physical presence at this meeting has great psychological importance, particularly for geographically dispersed teams, whose members may have few future opportunities to convene as a group. Being together at the very beginning of their long journey and getting to know each other at a personal level will help build commitment and bolster each participant's sense that this team and project are important. It's difficult to imagine anyone feeling part of a group with common goals without being in the physical presence of his or her teammates at some point. If certain people cannot attend the launch meeting because of their geographic location, every effort should be made to give them a virtual presence through videoconferencing or, at the very least, speakerphone.

The sponsor's presence at the launch meeting is imperative. His or her presence and demeanor speak volumes about the importance —or unimportance—ascribed to the project's mission. As experts Jon Katzenbach and Douglas Smith write:

> *When potential teams first gather, everyone monitors the signals given by others to confirm, suspend, or dispel assumptions and concerns. They pay particular attention to those in authority: the team leader and any executives who set up, oversee, or otherwise influence the team. And, as always, what such leaders do is more important than what they say. If a senior executive leaves the team kickoff to take a phone call ten minutes after the session has begun and he never returns, people get the message.*[1]

Here are tasks you should aim to accomplish at your project's official launch meeting:

- Be very clear about who belongs to the project team. Acknowledge each member by name if the group is not too large. There may be core members, and there may be peripheral members who participate for a limited time or in a limited way. But all are members. Do not tolerate any ambiguity on this point.

Welcome all those who will contribute to the project to the launch meeting.

- Explain the project charter and its contents. The sponsor or project manager should explain the goal, deliverables, and timetables as documented in the charter.

- Seek unanimous understanding of the charter. Just because the leadership explains the goal, deliverables, and so forth is no assurance that every team member will interpret them in the same way. Engage people in discussion about the charter with the goal of getting agreement and consensus.

- The sponsor should explain *why* the project's work is important and *how* its goals are aligned with larger organizational objectives. People need to know that they are part of something with important consequences for themselves and the organization; otherwise, they won't make their best effort. This discussion should aim to satisfy that need.

- Describe the resources available to the team and the nonteam personnel with whom members are likely to interact. That group may include other company employees, employees of alliance partners, suppliers, or customers.

- Describe team incentives. What, besides their normal compensation, will members receive if team goals are met or exceeded?

- Make introductions. Unless people are already familiar with each other and their special skills, use the launch meeting as an opportunity for personal introductions. If the group is of a reasonable size, ask participants to introduce themselves, to say something about their background and expertise, and to explain what they hope to contribute to the effort.

By the end of the launch meeting, people should have a clear sense of direction, the importance of the team goal to the organization, how success will be measured, and how they will be rewarded for their efforts. They should know who is on the team and what each is capable of contributing. And they should begin to think of themselves as members of a real team. A sense of belonging and contributing to a common goal can only develop with time and through shared experiences. Nevertheless, the seeds should be planted at the launch meeting.

Create Integrative Mechanisms

Simply throwing people into a launch meeting, giving them collective goals, and handing out free T-shirts with a team name and logo creates a team in name only. Effective project teams are created through collaborative activities: joint work, idea sharing, the give-and-take that typically surrounds important decisions, and exchanging information. A project manager can facilitate these team-building activities through integrative mechanisms.

Integrative mechanisms include regularly scheduled meetings, communications links such as newsletters, project Web sites, and the physical colocation of team members. Off-site social events can also be an effective strategy that builds team identification and group cohesion. Each of these mechanisms, in effect, encourages people to talk with one another, understand each other at a personal level, share ideas, analyze and critique alternative strategies, and build the bonds of trust and friendship that make team-based work stimulating and productive.

What integrative mechanisms is your project using?

Establish Norms of Behavior

Turning an assemblage of individuals into an effective project team cannot be done overnight. Individuals come to the effort with personal agendas. Many view their new teammates as competitors for promotions, recognition, and rewards. Still others may harbor personal grudges against one or more of the people with whom they have been thrown together. And there are always an individual or two who lack the social skills required for group work.

Personal agendas, internal competitions, grudges, and poor social skills are present to some degree on every team; they can undermine project effectiveness if they're not contained or neutralized. The diversity of specialties and work styles that you've probably brought to the team through great effort may also make collaboration more difficult. Technical specialists, for example, may speak an unfamiliar jargon, and that sets them apart from their teammates. And what people find unfamiliar they do not trust.

One of the best ways to manage these problems is to set down clear norms of behavior that apply equally to all. As described by Jon Katzenbach and Douglas Smith, authors of *The Wisdom of Teams*, a popular book on team-based work, the most critical rules pertain to:

- **Attendance**. Members and leaders must understand that the team cannot make decisions and accomplish its work if individual members fail to show up for meetings or joint work sessions. If you are the leader, people will follow your example. If you are chronically late or absent, they will mimic your behavior.

- **Interruptions**. Decide to turn cell phones off during meetings and work sessions. Taking a call during a team session indicates that the call is more important than what the team is doing. Also make it clear that people are not to interrupt others during meetings. Everyone has a right to speak.

- **No sacred cows**. Agree that no issues will be off-limits. For example, if a process-reengineering team knows that a change will upset a particular executive, its members should not be afraid or reluctant to discuss the issue. Avoiding the issue because of the executive's possible objections will signal that the team and its efforts are pointless.

- **Constructive criticism**. Problem solving is bound to produce competing solutions. The champions of these solutions must understand that they are empowered to represent their views but are forbidden to undermine those of others through deception or by withholding relevant data. Team players must also learn how to vent disagreement in constructive ways.

- **Confidentiality**. Some team issues are bound to be sensitive. Team members will not discuss those issues freely unless they are confident that what is said within the team stays within the team.

- **Action orientation**. Teams are not formed to meet and discuss; those that do are simply gab sessions that accomplish nothing. Their real purpose is to act and produce results. Make that clear from the very beginning. In the words of Katzenbach and Smith, an action-oriented team means that "everyone does real work" and "everyone gets assignments and does them."[2]

What should be your group's norms of behavior? That depends on the purpose of the group and the personalities of its members. But certainly any effective set of norms should be clear and concise. It should also include the basics: respect for all members of the group, a commitment to active listening, and an understanding about how to voice concerns and handle conflict.

To guarantee the free flow of ideas, some groups may want to go further—for example, making it explicit that anyone is entitled to disagree with anyone else. They may also want to adopt specific guidelines that

- support calculated risk taking,

- establish procedures about acknowledging and handling failure,

- foster individual expression, and

- encourage a playful attitude.

Whatever norms your group adopts, make sure all its members have a hand in establishing them—and that everyone agrees to abide by them. Members' participation and acceptance will head off many future problems. Also, be aware that norms sometimes emerge in unanticipated ways, even if guidelines are explicitly discussed at the beginning of the team project. For example, if some egos are bruised during the team's initial meetings, you may observe subtle hostility between the affected individuals in subsequent interactions. That hostility will probably manifest itself through second-guessing, criticism, sarcasm, and other counterproductive behaviors. As a leader or team member, you should discourage such actions, and remind everyone that mutual respect, open discussion, and collaborative behavior are the expected norms.

Summing Up

- Launch your project with an all-team meeting. Everyone should be there, including the sponsor. During that meeting, explain the charter. Stress the importance of the team's goals and how they fit with larger organizational goals.

- Integrative mechanisms help turn a group of individuals into a real team. Regularly scheduled meetings, communications links, physical colocation, and social events are mechanisms you can use to build team identification, group cohesion, and collaboration.

- You can smooth over incompatibilities and make the most of personal differences by creating norms of behavior and gaining their acceptance by others. Showing up at meetings on time, completing assignments on schedule, helping teammates when it's needed, constructive criticism, and respect for different viewpoints are examples of positive norms of behavior.

11

Keeping on Track

Maintaining Control

Key Topics Covered in This Chapter

- *Using budgets, quality checks, and milestones to monitor and control work*

- *Making the most of conflict*

- *Getting people to collaborate*

- *Communicating progress and possibilities*

- *Handling problems*

MANY OF THE concerns of project managers and project team leaders are the same concerns faced by managers in other situations: getting results through people and other resources. To accomplish their aims, managers and leaders must keep people motivated and focused on goals, mediate between the people above and the people below, and make decisions. They must also monitor and control adherence to schedule, budget, and quality standards; deal with people problems; and relentlessly facilitate communication.

This sounds like a big job—and it is! And it describes what project managers must do during the third phase of the project life cycle: managing execution. This chapter focuses on the three key responsibilities of project managers in this phase.

Monitoring and Controlling the Project

In some respects, the manager is analogous to the thermostat that monitors and controls the temperature in your house. Think for just a moment about how that thermostat functions. It is constantly sensing the temperature inside the building. If it senses that the air temperature is within a preset range, say 21 to 22 degrees Celsius, it thinks that all is well and does nothing. It takes action only if it senses a temperature outside of the desired range. If the temperature is too high, the thermostat signals the air-conditioning system to start working. If the temperature is too low, it signals the heating system to switch on. The thermostat continues monitoring the temperature, and once the building's temperature is back within the desired range, it sends another signal, telling the air conditioner or furnace to stop.

Management has analogous sensors and uses them to monitor activities under its control. It uses budgets to gauge the pace of spending relative to set targets, it checks the quality of output to sense whether work processes are functioning correctly, and it uses periodic milestones to assure itself that the work is on schedule. Let's examine each of these monitoring and control mechanisms.

The Budget

The basics of setting up a budget were presented earlier. Here we'll explain how you can use the budget to monitor project activities. Monitoring is accomplished by comparing the actual results for a given time period with the budget. If evaluation reveals that the project's spending is right on target, with actual results matching the budget's expected results, then no adjustment is required. However, if actual results differ from the expected results, then, simply put, the project manager must take corrective action. For example, if your team had expected to pay outside consultants $24,000 in July but you find that actual payments totaled $30,000, you need to investigate the reason for this discrepancy and possibly correct the situation.

The difference between actual results and the results expected by the budget is called a *variance*. A variance can be favorable, when the actual results are better than expected—or unfavorable, when the actual results are worse than expected. We see both favorable and unfavorable variances in table 11-1.

TABLE 11-1

Monthly Project Budget Report: July

Project Spending Categories	Actual Results	Budgeted Amounts	Variance
Supplies	$2,500	$2,000	+500; favorable
Outside consultants	$30,000	$24,000	−6,000; unfavorable
Travel	$9,000	$7,700	+1,300; favorable

Tips for Monitoring Budgets

When monitoring actual costs against your budget, watch out for these common factors; they can send your project over budget:

- Inflation during long-term projects

- Unfavorable changes in currency exchange rates

- Failing to get firm prices from suppliers and contractors

- Unplanned personnel costs, including overtime, incurred in keeping the project on schedule

- Unanticipated training costs and consulting fees

SOURCE: Harvard ManageMentor® on Project Management.

What should you do if monitoring detects unfavorable budget variances? One approach is a strategy of hope—that is, hope that the variance is simply a random deviation that will not repeat itself in the future. No smart manager will rely on that strategy. Overspending in one budget period, even to a moderate degree, may be a symptom of an underlying problem—one that will grow larger if left unattended. So when you see a significant budget variance, investigate. Why did it occur? Is it likely to repeat itself? What corrective measures are called for? As you address the problem, don't attempt to do it yourself; instead, enlist the people closest to the problem.

Quality Checks

Quality checks are another approach to keeping a project on track. They play an important role in every project, just as they do with normal work processes. In making a quality check, the project manager examines some unit of work at an appropriate point to assure that it meets specifications. For example, if the project is building a new e-commerce site, the project manager may want to test components of the software system as they are developed to assure that they function according to plan. She should not wait until the very end of the project to do this testing. By that time, any substandard work would cost enormous amounts of time and money to fix.

Periodic quality checks, like the building thermometer, indicate conditions that are out of specification. Once these problems are identified, the project team can find the cause of them and fix the processes that created them in the first place. That sort of monitoring and corrective action assures that subsequent task output will meet quality standards, keeping the project on track.

Milestones

Travelers in an earlier era used engraved stones encountered strategically along the road to assess their progress. "Cambridge: 17 Miles," one might read. The English-speaking world refers to these as milestones. We use figurative milestones to mark passages in our life: graduation from high school or college, marriage, the formation of one's own business, birthdays, and so forth. Projects use significant events as milestones to remind people of how far they have come and how much further they must go. These significant events may be the completion of key tasks on the critical path. Here are a few examples:

- The sponsor's acceptance of a complete set of customer requirements for a new service

- The successful testing of a product prototype

- Installation and successful testing of a critical piece of equipment

- Delivery of finished components to the stockroom

- And the ultimate milestone: completion of the project

Milestones should be highlighted in the project schedule and used to monitor progress. They should also be used as occasions for celebrating progress when celebration is called for. Some project teams recognize milestones with a group luncheon or a trip to a sporting event.

Strictly speaking, every task on the schedule represents a milestone, but some are more significant than others. The more significant markers have greater psychological appeal for team members. Use them to rally participants, and share words of encouragement like "We are now very close to completing the Web site's specifications. Let's keep up the pace and get it done on time."

Building a Suitable Monitoring/Control System

Budgets, quality checks, and milestones are basic monitoring and control devices that apply generally to projects. But there may be others that apply very specifically to your situation. Do you know what they are? If you don't, here is some advice for selecting and implementing them:

- **Focus on what is important**. You will need to continually ask questions like these: What is important to the organization? What are we attempting to do? Which parts of the project are the most important to track and control? What are the essential points at which controls need to be placed?

- **Build corrective action into the system**. Your control system, like the thermostat in our initial example, should emphasize response. If control data doesn't trigger a response, then your system is useless. Your system must use information to initiate corrective action; otherwise, all you are doing is monitoring and not exercising control. If quality is below standard, set up an ad hoc group to determine the cause, and fix the problem. Do the same if any of the project's teams have fallen behind schedule. Be very careful, however, that control doesn't lapse into micromanagement. Encourage the people closest to the problem to make the correction.

- **Emphasize timely responses**. Information must be received quickly for your responses to do any good. Ideally, you'll want real-time information. In most cases, though, weekly updates suffice.

Beware of Mission Creep

Throughout the project, be on guard against mission creep—unwittingly giving in to pressure to do more than has originally been planned for. As you find out each stakeholder's definition of success, you may feel pressure to accomplish too much. Don't get caught up in trying to solve problems that lie beyond the scope of your project—even legitimate or urgent problems that your company needs to address. For example, a project organized to develop and improve an automobile exhaust system should not get sidetracked into trying to develop more effective headlights. That's a different job requiring a very different set of skills. Remember: It's all right to change the project's objectives midstream, but do so with your eyes open, not unconsciously—and only after making sure all your stakeholders are willing to go along with the new objectives.

No single control system is right for all projects. A system that's right for a large project will swamp a small one with paperwork, while a system that works for small projects won't have enough muscle for a big one. So, find the one that's right for your project.

Dealing with People Issues

A quick scan of most popular books on project management would give you the impression that the subject is mostly about task analysis, measuring techniques, scheduling methods, and using software to plot and maintain a course. That impression, however, would be wrong. Yes, the techniques offered in this and other books are very useful. But people—particularly people working in teams—are at the heart of project work. People who labor and solve problems together, who share information, and who accept mutual responsibility for success or failure are much more important than mechanical techniques.

The people issues that matter for project work are extensive and are best addressed through books and training programs devoted to team management. Nevertheless, two key people issues are addressed here: conflict and collaboration. Both are necessary in keeping a project on track.

Mastering Conflict

One of the thorniest people issues faced by project managers is conflict among team members. Individuals brought together from different parts of an organization to complete a mission always present opportunities for conflict. Ironically, one of the important characteristics of a well-structured team—diversity of thinking, backgrounds, and skills—is itself a potential source of conflict. For example, engineering members of a product-development team may be impatient with the marketing specialist's concern with how customers will receive the new product. "We shouldn't be fixated with what customers want," they say. "If we build a better mousetrap, customers will beat a path to our door." "Not so," says the marketer. "We must get a better fix on customer requirements before moving forward." And so the conflict begins.

To turn conflict from a negative to a positive force, the project manager must encourage members to listen to each other, to be willing to understand different viewpoints, and to objectively question each other's assumptions. At the same time, the project manager must prevent conflict from becoming personal or from going underground, where resentment simmers. Here are three steps for making the most of conflict:

1. **Create a climate that encourages people to discuss difficult issues**. Disagreement builds and produces no positive results when people fail to deal with the conflict's source. Some people call this matter "the moose on the table." It's there, but nobody wants to acknowledge it or to talk about it. Make it clear that you *want* the tough issues aired, and that *anyone* can point out a moose.

2. **Facilitate the discussion**. How do you deal with a moose once it has been identified? Use the following guidelines:

- First, acknowledge the issue, even if only one person sees it.

- Refer back to group norms on how people have agreed to treat each other.

- Encourage the person who identified the moose to be specific: What, exactly, do you see as the problem here? How is that problem affecting our work as a team?

- Keep the discussion impersonal. Do not assign blame. Instead, discuss *what* is impeding progress, not *who*.

- If the issue involves someone's behavior, encourage the person who identified the problem to explain how that behavior affects him or her, rather than to make assumptions about the motivation behind the behavior. For example, if someone is not completing work on time, you might say, "When your work is delivered late, the rest of us are unable to meet our deadlines," not "I know you are not really excited about this product, but that shouldn't be an excuse for wrecking our schedule." Likewise, if someone is chronically late for scheduled meetings, don't say, "What makes you think that you are so important that you can show up late for meetings?" Instead, try something like this: "Your being late for meetings means that we cannot start on schedule. That wastes the time of five or six other people and prevents us from completing our meeting agendas."

- Team members should also know how to give feedback to the project manager. If they sense a lack of leadership, they might say, "When you don't provide us with direction, we have to guess what you want. If we guess wrong, we waste lots of time," not "You don't seem to have any idea what we should be doing on this project." A good manager knows how to receive feedback, even when it's negative.

3. **Move toward closure on conflict by discussing what can be done**.

- Leave meetings with concrete suggestions for improvement, if not a solution to the problem.

- If the subject is too sensitive and discussions are going nowhere, adjourn your meeting until a specified date so that people can cool down. Or, bring in a facilitator. A good facilitator can help warring parties settle their differences in a positive way.

Generating Collaborative Behavior

Collaboration is the bedrock of team effectiveness. It makes a team greater than the sum of its parts. But collaboration doesn't always occur naturally.

Have you ever watched a basketball game in which one player took a shot just about every time he got his hands on the ball? His teammates passed the ball whenever they were badly positioned or closely guarded by opposing players. But the "ball hog" never passed, even when a teammate was within easy striking distance of the basket. This is one type of noncollaborative behavior you have to watch for on your project team. Why? Because noncollaborative behavior will slow down your project.

Specifically, check to see whether team members are sharing the work or whether one person is trying to do it all. Even if this prima donna is a high performer, his or her behavior will discourage participation by others and slow overall progress. Also, watch for anyone, including a team leader, who

- appears to be taking undue credit for the team's accomplishment,

- is always pressing to get a larger share of team resources,

- is secretive or unwilling to share information, or

- turns disagreements over goals or methods into personal conflicts.

That last point deserves special attention because personal animosity will throw your project off track. According to team expert Jeffrey Polzer, relationship conflict distracts people from their work and causes them to reduce their commitment to the team and its goals. "Some teams can't get through a meeting without an angry outburst, overt criticism, and hard feelings," he writes. When this happens, team members may respond by withdrawing from debates, attempting instead to preserve their relationships by avoiding confrontation.[1]

Tips for Making the Most of People

If you are a project manager or team leader, you will be more successful in reaching your milestones if you adopt this advice about dealing with people:

- Be very selective in recruiting. Bring in people who view the project's goals as important. These people will be more predisposed to concentrating on achieving goals than to thinking about the differences they have with other team members.

- Engage members in activities they find interesting and valuable. This too will keep them focused on results.

- Publicly recognize the contributions of individual members. Doing so will make them feel appreciated, valued, and part of the group.

- Recognize the value of differences and how they serve the common goal. Unique skills and singular insights contribute to success.

- Create opportunities for members to know each other. Whether it's through off-site recreation, lunches in the team room, or something else, give people opportunities to get to know each other at a personal level. Doing so will help them cut through stereotypes (like, "those finance people are hard to work with") and find bases for collaboration.

- Get people working together! Working together side by side can build team spirit.

If you observe this kind of relationship conflict, take action to stop it. Do whatever is necessary to bring the feuding parties together, to examine the conflict in an objective manner, and to seek a resolution. If either or both parties are too stubborn or too single-minded to work things out, think about getting those individuals off the project.

Note: Conflict and collaboration are not the only people problems that a manager must address in keeping a project on track. There can also be problems associated with the team structure, individual team members, and the quality of work. For solutions to those problems, check table 11-2.

The Role of Communication

We've already explored the importance of creating a communications plan as part of the larger project management process. Meetings, newsletters, reports, and one-on-one encounters are mechanisms for disseminating information, sharing ideas, and encouraging productive dialogue. They also help projects stay on track.

To understand how to use communications to keep a project on track, think about the information that different project participants need to accomplish their missions.

- **The sponsor.** The sponsor needs periodic status, or progress, reports from the project manager. These should indicate where the project and its various initiatives stand relative to the schedule, the budget, and quality measures. A written report is the usual medium of communicating this information. (Note: Appendix A at the back of this book contains a sample project progress report.) The sponsor will also want to know about current and anticipated problems, change requests, and new opportunities discovered in the course of project work. Regular meetings are the best way to report these issues. The sponsor can use the meetings to guide the manager and authorize certain activities.

- **The project manager**. In a sizable project, the manager must delegate substantial responsibility to one or more team leaders. There may be, for instance, a team leader in charge of technical activities, another for marketing initiatives, and so forth. The project manager will look to these leaders for the same type of reporting that he or she provides to the sponsor. Once again, regular progress reports and meetings are used to share information, authorize action, make decisions, and keep the project on track.

- **Project team members**. Project managers and team leaders use communications to direct and control activities with team members. Individual members can inform management about barriers to progress, newly discovered opportunities, and where best to direct resources. But communication must be a two-way street. Team members need to know the general status of the project, what decisions have been made that affect their work, and how they should proceed in ambiguous situations. Meetings are generally the best forums for these information exchanges.

- **Stakeholders**. A sound stakeholder communications system is also important. These people will want continuous updates on project status and progress.

Handling Problems

A big part of keeping a project on track is handling the myriad problems that inevitably surface. A manager or scientist agitates for expansion of the project's mission. Several tasks take longer to complete than expected. Two team leaders fight over resources, splitting team members into hostile camps. Like pestering mosquitoes, problems like those can eat up your time and attention. Because it is impossible to provide advice about each of these problems in a book of this size, we've included a troubleshooting guide, table 11-2.

TABLE 11-2

Troubleshooting Guide

Problem	Possible Causes	Potential Impact	Recommended Action
Team Structure Problems			
Team member leaves	• Didn't get along with teammates	• Impact may be slight if a new person with the same skills can be recruited • Could create a crisis if you cannot find a person with the same skills	• Create backups for this and other key positions • Cross-train team members • Use the opportunity to bring in a person with even more know-how • Avoid the problem by having backups for key positions
Lack of skills/missing skills	• Certain skills overlooked during planning • Need for new skills discovered in the middle of the project • Organization was not prepared to take on the project	• The project will not move forward as fast as it should or it might stall	• Have team member trained in the needed skill • Hire outside consultants or contractors who have the skill
Interpersonal Problems			
Inflexible team members	• People think that their way is the only way to operate • Anxiety over trying new approaches	• Progress slowed or blocked	• Indicate your expectation of flexibility at the very beginning • Work one-on-one to reduce anxiety over using new approaches • Look for flexibility when recruiting members
Conflict within the team	• Different working styles and areas of expertise • People are not prepared by training or experience for team-based work	• Progress, commitment to goals, and team cohesiveness will suffer	• Get people to focus on project goals and solutions • Build commitment to goals • Break up cliques • Counsel or remove agitators from the project

Problem	Possible Causes	Potential Impact	Recommended Action
Productivity Problems			
Time wasted on wrong tasks	• Poor time management • People are not prioritizing tasks • Weak management	• Tasks on the critical path will suffer	• Manager should make priorities clear
Poor quality work	• Quality standards not understood • Inadequate skills	• Project will fail to meet expectations of stakeholders • Costly and time-consuming rework will delay the project	• Recruit people who have the skills required to produce the requisite quality • Apply skill training where needed • Managers should communicate quality expectations from the very beginning
Team member burnout	• Schedulers have overcommitted members • Failure to create jobs with sufficient variety • Failure to communicate the importance of tasks	• Schedule delays • Poor quality work • Poor morale	• Avoid overscheduling individuals • Communicate the importance of key tasks • Build variety and learning into job assignments
Schedule Problems			
Tasks are falling behind schedule	• Miscalculated task durations in the planning stage • Reason for schedule problem unknown	• Will continue to get worse, putting the project further and further behind schedule	• Face up to the planning miscalculation, and readjust the schedule if possible • Create and implement a solution to the problem and then monitor progress very closely • Working with people closest to the problem, seek the cause

Source: Harvard ManageMentor® on Project Management (Boston: Harvard Business School Publishing, 2002), 42–44. Adapted with permission.

Projects generally experience four classes of conflicts: team-structure problems, interpersonal problems, productivity problems, and schedule problems. The troubleshooting guide identifies some fairly typical issues, their possible causes, their potential impact, and recommended action. Though it is by no means complete, you may find it useful.

Summing Up

• Budgets are useful tools in controlling and tracking project performance. Variances point to areas where you should intervene or investigate.

• Conduct periodic quality checks to identify problems; then find and deal with the causes.

• Use completed milestones as opportunities to celebrate project progress.

• Watch out for diversity; it is both a source of strength and potential conflict.

• Discourage conflict and noncollaborative behavior.

• Use your communications system to sense problems and signal responses.

12

The Closedown Phase

Wrapping It Up

Topics Covered in This Chapter

- *The value of the project closedown phase*

- *How to evaluate a finished project*

- *Documenting project work for future learning*

- *Using a special session to capture and pass along lessons learned*

- *Capping the project with a celebration*

CLOSEDOWN should be the final phase of every project. At this point, the team delivers, or reports, its results to the sponsor and stakeholders and then examines its own performance. Managers are inclined to gloss over this phase since they are generally unaccustomed to closedown activities. After all, their regular jobs are ongoing. And being action-oriented people, they're eager to move on without looking back once a job is finished.

Closedown is worth doing despite the habits of busy managers. It helps people through the psychological issues that go hand-in-hand with important work-life transitions, and it is particularly important when team members have devoted themselves to a project for long periods of time. Closedown provides an opportunity to thank people who have contributed—both team members and the many other individuals who supplied advice and resources at some point in the project's life.

More important, the closedown phase gives everyone a chance to reflect on what has been accomplished, what went right, what went wrong, and how the outcome might have been improved. Such reflections are at the core of organizational learning—learning that can and should be shared with other projects sponsored by the organization.

The closedown activities examined here are performance evaluations, documentation, lessons learned, and celebration.

Not All Projects Have a Clear Ending

We generally think of projects as having a clear beginning, a period of work, and a clear closedown. But not every project fits that tidy mold. Some simply move from one phase to another. A software-development project that has finalized version 1.0, for example, may shift immediately to planning and work on version 2.0. The same project many assign some of its people to the development of patches for the version it has just shipped. Even in such instances, however, closing the books on the initial project should coincide with the closedown activities explained in this chapter.

Performance Evaluation

Performance evaluation is concerned with how well the project performed relative to the three key factors included in its charter and any subsequent amendments:

- **Objectives or deliverables**. Have all objectives been met? Have project deliverables met the mandated specifications? For example, if the charter required the delivery of a complete plan for entering a new market, including data on market size, a listing of competing products and prices, and so forth, the plan submitted by the project should be evaluated against each of those details.

- **Schedule**. Did the project complete its work on time? If it did not, the project team should do two things: (1) estimate the cost of its tardiness to the company and (2) determine the cause of the schedule delay and how could it have been prevented.

- **Cost**. What did it cost to complete the project? Was that cost within budget constraints? If the project ran over budget, the team should determine the cause of overspending and how that variance might have been avoided.

Ideally, an independent party that's capable of making an objective assessment should participate in postproject evaluation.

Documentation

Every large project produces reams of documents, such as meeting minutes, budget data, the closedown performance evaluation, and so on. These documents are part of the historical record; they should be collected and stored.

Why bother with documentation? It's a source of learning. Consider this example:

> *The market strategy project finished its work two years ago and did a praiseworthy job. Its deliverable—a complete market analysis and plan for introducing a new breakfast cereal—was credited with the successful launch of CornCrunchies.*
>
> *Now Helen, a young product manager at the same company, has been given the job of organizing and leading an analogous project, this one aimed at introducing KiddieKrunchies, another breakfast food under development. Not wanting to re-invent the wheel, Helen and core members of her project hope to learn from the CornCrunchies experience. "Let's see how that team organized and scheduled work and how it tracked progress," she suggests.*
>
> *And so Helen and her team spent several days poring through the stored documents of that earlier project. They picked out useful reporting templates, research reports, and Gantt charts. They also interviewed the CornCrunchies project manager and several key participants. "This information will make our planning phase much easier," she thought.*
>
> *Then one of Helen's coworkers, Stephen, made an important discovery. "A report I found in the file cites a meeting between our marketing people and Fieldfresh, a major UK grocery distributor," he said. "According to this report, Fieldfresh had proposed being the exclusive*

*UK distributor for CornCrunchies, but our people went with Manches-
ter Foods instead."*

*"And we all know what a poor job Manchester has done in the
UK," Helen chimed in. "Make a copy of that report, Stephen. We'll
want to have Fieldfresh on our list of possible distributors."*

In this case, Helen's team found several useful things in the previous
project's documentation: a proven approach to organizing work
around marketing analysis and planning; reporting forms; and a potential overseas distributor. Your project may likewise be a gold mine
of useful information for subsequent project teams—but only if you
gather together all important documents and store them in accessible formats.

Lessons Learned

Writing in the *Harvard Business Review*, Frank Gulliver identified
learning as one of the important values of project work—a value overlooked by many. "If your company is like most," he writes, "you spend
thousands of hours planning an investment, millions of dollars implementing it—and nothing evaluating and learning from it."[1] Not every
organization is that shortsighted. The U.S. Army has maintained its
Center for Army Lessons Learned for decades. The center's mission is
to learn whatever it can from every type of combat operation and turn
that learning into practical advice that it then disseminates to soldiers
in the field. It actively solicits input from battle-tested soldiers on
everything from urban warfare maneuvers, to when and when not to
wear body armor, to the effectiveness of high-tech systems under adverse field conditions, as experienced in mountainous Afghanistan.

The center also looks outside the army's own experience for important lessons. One article on its Web site, for example, documents
and evaluates the tactics used by Chechen rebels in the embattled
city of Grozny and the problems that Russian forces had in dealing
with those insurgents. (See http://call.army.mil for the Center for
Army Lessons Learned.)

Most businesspeople believe that they are light-years ahead of the military in matters of management. But lessons learned is one area in which private industry can learn a lesson of its own. And plenty of those lessons can be found in project team operations and their supporting reports.

Lessons learned should be part of every closedown operation. Project participants should convene to identify what went right and what went wrong. They should make a list of their successes, their mistakes, their unjustified assumptions, and things that could have been done better. That list should become part of the documented record.

Four Lessons

In an article in *Harvard Business Review*, Frank Gulliver points to four main lessons that he and British Petroleum learned through systematic postproject appraisals (PPA). These are:

1. **Determine cost more accurately.** Prior to PPA, BP planners inaccurately predicted the scope of their projects. In most cases, this led to unrealistically low project budgets.

2. **Anticipate and minimize risk.** The company learned from its experience with acquisitions and plant expansions that project planners should take the extra time needed to study market issues.

3. **Evaluate contractors.** PPA led to the establishment of a contractor evaluation unit dedicated to judging contractor qualifications and monitoring their performance.

4. **Improve project management.** At the recommendation of PPA, the company set up a projects department to help its engineers develop the know-how to become skilled project managers.

SOURCE: Frank R. Gulliver, "Post-Project Appraisals Pays," *Harvard Business Review*, March–April 1987, 128–130.

Here is a partial list of questions that should be addressed at a lessons learned session:

- In retrospect, how sound were our assumptions?

- Did we bother to test key assumptions?

- How well did we seek out alternatives?

- What about our time estimates—did we under- or overestimate task duration?

- Were our meetings productive or time wasters?

And the ultimate question: If we could start over again tomorrow, which things would we change?

Make a systematic list of these lessons, grouped by topic (for example, planning, budgeting, execution, and so forth) and organized in a form similar to table 12-1. Make that document available to all subsequent project teams. Next to the deliverables, these lessons may be the most valuable output of your project experience.

TABLE 12-1

Project Lessons Learned

Project Phase/Task	What Worked	What Didn't Work	Ways to Improve
Planning/time estimates		Consistently under-estimated time to complete tasks. Wrecked our schedule.	Must be more systematic in making estimates. No more top-of-the-head guesses. Get expert advice.
Execution/budget control	Biweekly budget reporting identified variances before they could get out of hand.		Underestimated the budget for out-sourced software development. Next time include one of our internal IT people on the team.

Source: Harvard ManageMentor® on Project Management (Boston: Harvard Business School Publishing, 2002), 54. Used with permission.

Putting Learning to Work

One way that you can put learned lessons to work is to establish staffing continuity between the projects your company launches. For example, if the company has just completed one software-development project, make sure that, skill requirements permitting, several veterans of that project are assigned to the next one. These veterans will bring lessons from the first project with them and will be sources of experience and know-how for first-time project members.

Celebration

If you followed the advice given earlier, you formally began your project with a launch meeting and perhaps some attendant festivities. The sponsor attended that event and drew a mental picture of the journey you were about to begin and what the project aimed to accomplish. The CEO was present to explain the importance of the project to the company and to all of its employees.

In closing down the project, do something very similar, with the same cast of characters reflecting back on what you've done and on the project's impact on the company. If the project was a success, be sure to invite whichever customers, suppliers, and nonproject employees helped during the journey. If the project failed to deliver on its entire list of objectives, highlight the effort that people made and the goals they did achieve.

The project manager should use the occasion to thank all who helped and participated. Once that's done, it's time to pull the corks and celebrate the end of your project.

Summing Up

- Evaluate project performance on the basis of chartered objectives or deliverables and adherence to schedule and cost.

- Project documentation creates a record for future learning.

- At the end of the project, use an informal meeting to dredge up the many things that led to success and failure. Make a systematic list of those items and make it available to future project personnel.

- Use a closedown meeting to make the formal end of the project, to celebrate successes, to recount lessons, and to thank all participants.

Useful Implementation Tools

This appendix contains a number of tools that can help you be more effective in forming a team, managing its progress, and handling typical problems. All the forms are adapted from Harvard ManageMentor, an online product of Harvard Business School Publishing.

1. **Defining Your Project (figure A-1).** This form will help you uncover the issues and parameters at the core of your project.

2. **Work Breakdown Structure (figure A-2).** Use this form to develop a Work Breakdown Structure to ensure that you do not overlook a significant part of a complex activity or underestimate the time and money needed to complete the work. Use multiple pages as needed.

3. **Project Progress Report (figure A-3).** Use this form to help assess progress, present information to others, and think through next steps. For the convenience of readers, a downloadable version of this tool can be found on the Harvard Business Essentials series Web site: www.elearning.hbsp.org/businesstools.

FIGURE A-1

Defining Your Project

UNCOVER THE ISSUES AND PARAMETERS AT THE CORE OF YOUR PROJECT.

The "real" project
What is the perceived need or purpose for what we are trying to do?
What caused people to see this as a problem that needed to be solved?
What criteria are people going to use to judge this project a success?

The stakeholders
Who has a stake in the solution or outcome?
How do the various stakeholders' goals for the project differ?
What functions or people might the project's activities or outcomes affect?
Who is going to contribute resources (people, space, time, tools, money)?

Skills required for the project	
Skill Needed	Possible Team Member
1.	1.
2.	2.
3.	3.
4.	4.
5.	5.
6.	6.

Source: Harvard ManageMentor® on Project Management (Boston: Harvard Business School Publishing, 2002), 50. Used with permission.

FIGURE A-2

Work Breakdown Structure

Describe the overall project:			
Major Task	**Level 1 Subtasks**	**Level 2 Subtasks**	**Level 2 Subtask Duration**

Total duration (hours/weeks/days)

Major Task	**Level 1 Subtasks**	**Level 2 Subtasks**	**Level 2 Subtask Duration**

Total duration (hours/weeks/days)

Source: Harvard ManageMentor® on Project Management (Boston: Harvard Business School Publishing, 2002), 51. Used with permission.

FIGURE A-3

Project Progress Report

Project:	**Prepared by:**
For the period from:	**To:**

Current Status

Key milestones for this period:	
Achieved (list)	Coming up next (list)

Key issues or problems:	
Resolved (list)	Need to be resolved (list)

Key decisions:			
Made (list)	Need to be made (list)	By whom	When

Budget status:

Implications
List changes in objectives, timeline/delivery dates, project scope, and resource allocation (including people and financial).

Next steps		
List the specific action steps that will be done to help move this project forward successfully. Put a name and date next to each step if possible.		
Step	Person responsible	Date

Comments:

Source: Harvard ManageMentor® on Project Management (Boston: Harvard Business School Publishing, 2002), 52. Used with permission.

A Guide to Effective Meetings

Meetings are a fact of life in most organizational work, and equally so with projects. Because they are so frequent and so important, it's in the project's interests to make those meetings as effective as possible. You can conduct effective meetings if you pay attention to these key aspects of meetings: preparation, the meeting process itself, and follow-up. This guide is adapted from Harvard ManageMentor, an online product of Harvard Business School Publishing.

Be Prepared

You've undoubtedly attended meetings for which there was little or no preparation. Did those meetings accomplish anything? Probably not. In some cases, the purpose of the meeting was unclear from the beginning. In others, one or more of the people needed to make a decision didn't receive an invitation. You can avoid such mistakes by following these commonsense rules:

- Make sure that your meetings are necessary. Meetings eat up time for everyone at the table. If you can accomplish your objective without calling a meeting, do so.

- Clarify every meeting's objective. Every attendee should be able to answer this question: Why am I here? If the objective is to make a decision, be sure that everyone understands this in advance, and that they have the time and materials needed to prepare.

- Involve the right people. Invite only those who have something to contribute, whose participation is necessary, or who can learn from the discussion.

- Provide an agenda in advance. An agenda indirectly identifies the meeting's objective.

- Sound out key participants in advance. You'll be better prepared for a meeting if you know in advance what key participants think about important items on the agenda. What you learn may suggest an alteration in the agenda.

- Insist that people be prepared. This means being up to speed on the issues; bringing relevant documents, reports, or physical objects; and being ready to contribute to the discussion and a decision.

During the Meeting

Good preparation will set you up for this second stage. Here you should:

- State the meeting's purpose. Even though you said it already when you invited people to the meeting, it's always smart to reiterate the meeting's purpose.

- Let everyone have a say. If one or two individuals are dominating the conversation, or if certain attendees are shy about leaping in, say, "Thanks for those ideas, Phil. What are your thoughts about this problem, Charlotte?"

- Keep the discussion from wandering. Meetings that wander off the key issues quickly degenerate into time-wasting gab sessions.

- End with confirmation and an action plan. Your meeting should transition to some action. "OK, we've decided to hire DataWhack to install the new servers. And, as agreed, I will obtain the purchase order, Bill will phone the salesperson and set up the schedule, and Janet will begin looking for someone to take the old equipment off our hands."

Follow–Up

Once a meeting is over, we're all tempted to relax and say, "I'm glad that's over with." But it isn't over if you led the meeting or agreed to accept responsibility for actions emanating from it.

The meeting leader should rapidly follow up with a quick memo in the same spirit as this one:

From: Richard

To: The IT Project Team

Thanks for your contributions to this morning's meeting. We have selected DataWhack as the supplier for the new servers. I view this as a good choice and a decision that moves us one step closer to the completion of our project. The action steps from this decision are as follows:

- *I will obtain the purchase order.*
- *Bill will contact the salesperson about the schedule.*
- *Janet will begin looking for someone to take the old servers off our hands.*

Let's complete these chores this week. Then we can get on to the next scheduled task.

This type of follow-up memo encourages people by saying that they are one step closer to their goal, and it reminds certain attendees about the action steps to which they have agreed.

Notes

Chapter 1

1. Lynda M. Applegate, Robert D. Austin, and F. Warren McFarlan, *Corporate Information Strategy and Management*, 6th ed. (Burr Ridge, IL: McGraw-Hill/Irwin, 2002), 278.

2. Gregory H. Watson, *Strategic Benchmarking* (New York: John Wiley & Sons, Inc., 1993), 114–115.

3. For a discussion of heavyweight and lightweight leaders and core teams, see Steven C. Wheelwright and Kim B. Clark, *Leading Product Development* (New York: Free Press, 1995), 81–85.

Chapter 2

1. Richard Leifer, Christopher McDermott, Gina Colarelli O'Connor, Lois Peters, Mark Rice, and Robert Veryzer, *Radical Innovation* (Boston: Harvard Business School Press, 2000), 163.

2. Jeffrey T. Polzer, "Leading Teams," Class note N9-403-094 (Boston: Harvard Business School, 2002), 7.

3. Jon R. Katzenbach and Douglas K. Smith, "The Wisdom of Teams," *Harvard Business Review*, March–April 1993, 118.

4. The essential characteristics listed here are largely drawn from two important trains of thought on teams. Competence and commitment to a common goal reflect the work of Jon R. Katzenbach and Douglas K. Smith, whose popular book *The Wisdom of Teams* appeared in 1993. J. Richard Hackman is the source for two other key characteristics of team success: an enabling structure and a supportive environment. Hackman's *Leading Teams* was published in 2002. For other important ideas about teams and their management, see the list of books and articles in "For Further Reading" at the end of this book.

5. For a discussion of heavyweight teams and team leaders, see Steven C. Wheelwright and Kim B. Clark, *Leading Product Development* (New York: Free Press, 1995), 81–85.

Chapter 3

1. J. Richard Hackman, *Leading Teams* (Boston: Harvard Business School Press, 2002), 83

2. Ibid., 74.

Chapter 4

1. Thomas J. Allen, "Communication Networks in R&D Labs," *R&D Management* 1 (1971): 14–21.

2. Marc H. Meyer and Alvin P. Lehnerd, *The Power of Product Platforms* (New York: Free Press, 1997), 137.

Chapter 9

1. Robert D. Austin, "Project Management and Discovery," *Science*'s Next Wave, 12 September 2002, <http://nextwave.sciencemag.org/cgi/content/full/2002/09/10/4> (accessed 4 September 2003).

2. See Robert Austin, "The Effects of Time Pressure on Quality in Software Development: An Agency Model," *Information Systems Research* 12, no. 2 (2001): 195–207.

3. Lynda M. Applegate, Robert D. Austin, and F. Warren McFarlan, *Corporate Information Strategy and Management*, 6th ed. (Burr Ridge, IL: McGraw-Hill/Irwin, 2003), 269–270.

4. Robert Austin, "Project Management and Discovery," *Science*'s Next Wave, 12 September 2002, <http://nextwave.sciencemag.org/cgi/content/full/2002/09/10/4> (accessed 4 September 2003).

Chapter 10

1. Jon R. Katzenbach and Douglas K. Smith, "The Discipline of Teams," *Harvard Business Review*, March–April 1993, 118.

2. Ibid.

Chapter 11

1. Jeffrey T. Polzer, "Leading Teams," Class note N9-403-094 (Boston: Harvard Business School, 2002), 15.

Chapter 12

1. Frank R. Gulliver, "Post-Project Appraisals Pay," *Harvard Business Review*, March–April 1987, 128–130.

Glossary

BOTTLENECK Any task on the critical path that causes the work feeding it to pile up.

BUDGET The translation of plans into measurable expenditures and anticipated returns over a certain period of time.

CHARTER A concise written description of the project's intended work. The charter may contain the name of the sponsor, a timetable, a description of deliverables, the benefits to the company, and a budget.

COACHING A two-way activity in which the parties share knowledge and experience in order to maximize a team member's potential and help him or her achieve agreed-upon goals. It is a shared effort in which the person being coached participates actively and willingly.

CONTINGENCY PLAN A course of action prepared in advance of a potential problem; it answers this question: "If X happens, how can we respond in an effective way?"

CRITICAL PATH METHOD A planning technique used for complex projects that consist of several individual activities. If one or more of the activities need to be completed before others can move forward, then those activities are called "critical"—and necessary for the on-time success of the project. The total duration of the project is defined by the critical path.

FACILITATOR A person, usually a consultant or human resource trainer, who helps team members to work together effectively.

FINISH-TO-START A task relationship in which one task must finish before the other can begin.

GANTT CHART A bar chart with tasks listed in the left-hand column and fitted into appropriate time blocks. These blocks indicate when a task should begin, based on task relationships, and when they should end.

165

INTERPERSONAL SKILL   The ability to work effectively with others—a very important trait for team-based work.

LAGGING   A task relationship in which one task must await the start and partial completion of another.

NETWORK DIAGRAM   A scheduling chart that reveals all the dependent relationships between tasks. It also reveals the critical path. Generally synonymous with a PERT chart.

ORGANIZATIONAL SKILL   The ability to communicate with other units, knowledge of the political landscape of the company, and possession of a network.

PERFORMANCE EVALUATION AND REVIEW TECHNIQUE (PERT)   A scheduling method that, when charted, represents every task as a node that connects with other nodes required to complete the project. A PERT chart may have many parallel or interconnecting networks of tasks so that periodic reviews are encouraged for complex projects. Unlike the Gantt chart, it indicates all the important task relationships and project milestones.

PROBLEM-SOLVING SKILL   An individual's ability to analyze difficult situations or impasses and to craft solutions.

PROJECT   A set of activities that (1) aims to produce a unique deliverable (for example, a new commercial airframe) and (2) is time bound within a clear beginning and ending point.

PROJECT MANAGEMENT   The allocation, tracking, and utilization of resources to achieve a particular objective within a specified period of time.

PROJECT MANAGER   The individual charged with planning and scheduling project tasks and with day-to-day management of project execution.

PROJECT STEERING COMMITTEE   A project entity that approves the project charter, secures resources, and adjudicates all requests to change key project elements, including deliverables, schedule, and budget.

PROJECT TEAM   A team organized around a nonroutine task of limited duration.

RISK MANAGEMENT   The part of the project planning process that identifies the key risks and develops plans to prevent them and/or mitigate the adverse effects of their occurrence.

SPONSOR   A manager or executive who has a stake in a team's outcome and the authority to define and approve its work.

STAKEHOLDER   Anyone who has a vested interest in the outcome of a project, who will judge a project's success or failure.

STEERING COMMITTEE   See *project steering committee.*

TEAM ROOM   A physical space dedicated to project team work. The team room is used for meetings, informal gatherings, and the display and storage of artifacts and documents that are central to the team's mission.

TECHNICAL SKILL   Specific expertise—in market research, finance, software programming, and so forth. Usually acquired through special training or education.

VARIANCE   The difference between actual results and expected results in the budget. Variance can be favorable or unfavorable. Managers use variance to spot sources of trouble and exceptional performance.

WORK BREAKDOWN STRUCTURE (WBS)   A planning routine that decomposes a project's goal into the many tasks required to achieve it. The time and money needed to complete those tasks are then estimated.

For Further Reading

Notes and Articles

Gulliver, Frank R. "Post-Project Appraisals Pay." *Harvard Business Review*, March–April 1987. British Petroleum (BP) began operating a postproject appraisal unit—a team of inside analysts and investigators who scrutinized projects several years after they had been completed to learn why they succeeded or misfired. The author explains how the appraisal process has helped managers be more accurate in developing project proposals and more efficient in implementing them. He also indicates that every BP project generated a return on investment at least as high as that in the project's forecast.

Harvard Business School Publishing. *Project Management Manual*. Boston: Harvard Business School Publishing, 2002. A brief primer on getting a project organized and managing it to completion.

Pinto, Jeffrey K., and Om P. Kharbanda. "How to Fail in Project Management (Without Really Trying)." *Business Horizons*, July–August 1996, 45–53. Project management techniques have met with widespread acceptance as a means of expediting product development, making efficient use of resources, and stimulating cross-functional communication. Not only manufacturing firms, but also legal offices, hospitals, and local governments have accepted project management as an indispensable part of their operations. Yet failures and outright disasters abound. A study of these unsuccessful attempts by these authors indicates a dozen surefire methods for dooming a project.

"What You Can Learn from Professional Project Managers," *Harvard Management Update*, February 2001. Companies that manage large-capital projects or a multitude of simultaneous projects have long recognized the need for expertise in the techniques of planning, scheduling, and controlling work. But over the past decade, non–project-driven firms—

especially those that see themselves as selling solutions rather than prod-ucts—have seen the light too. As a result, project management has be-come increasingly important and complex. This article outlines how they can benefit from the professionalism of the field.

Books

Frame, J. Davidson. *The Project Management Competence: Building Key Skills for Individuals, Teams, and Organizations.* San Francisco: Jossey-Bass, 1999. Like other management arts, effective project management requires skill at the individual, team, and organizational level. This book shows how project management skill at those levels dovetails to achieve successful outcomes. It explains the competencies needed by project managers and how they must be supported by the larger organization.

Kerzner, Harold. *Applied Project Management: Best Practices on Implementa-tion.* New York: John Wiley & Sons, Inc., 2000. This book offers com-mentaries from managers on their decision-making processes, including their successes and failures, in project management implementation. Twenty-five case studies highlight important project management is-sues, problems, and their solutions. Also included are commentaries on benchmarked best practices.

Mingus, Nancy. *Alpha Teach Yourself Project Management in 24 Hours.* Indi-anapolis, IN: Alpha Books, 2002. A step-by-step guide of 24 lessons for building and managing a project.

Schmaltz, David A. *The Blind Man and the Elephant.* San Francisco: Berrett-Koehler Publishers, Inc., 2003. Using the familiar metaphor of six blind men who fail to describe an elephant to each other, this author seeks out the cause of difficulties in project work. That cause, in his finding, is the inability of a group of coworkers to create common meaning from their common project experience.

Index

About the Subject Adviser

ROBERT D. AUSTIN is a member of the Technology and Operations Management faculty at the Harvard Business School. His extensive experience managing real projects came as an executive in a new business being created by a prominent technology firm, and also during ten years at the Ford Motor Company.

Professor Austin's research focuses on management of nonrepetitive, knowledge-intensive activities and on information technology management. He is the author of four books: *Artful Making: What Managers Need to Know About How Artists Work* (coauthored with Lee Devin, 2003), *Corporate Information Strategy and Management* (coauthored with Lynda M. Applegate and F. Warren McFarlan, 2003), *Creating Business Advantage in the Information Age* (also coauthored with Applegate and McFarlan, 2002), and *Measuring and Managing Performance in Organizations* (1996).

About the Writer

RICHARD LUECKE is the writer of this and several other books in the Harvard Business Essentials series. Based in Salem, Massachusetts, Mr. Luecke has authored or developed more than thirty books and dozens of articles on a wide range of business subjects. He has an M.B.A. from the University of St. Thomas.

Need smart, actionable management advice?

Look no further than your desktop.

Harvard ManageMentor®, a popular online performance support tool from Harvard Business School Publishing, brings how-to guidance and advice to your desktop, ready when you need it, on a host of issues critical to your work. Now available in a PLUS version with audio-enhanced practice exercises.

Heading up a team? Resolving a conflict between employees? Preparing a make-or-break presentation for a client? Setting next year's budget? Harvard ManageMentor delivers practical advice, tips, and tools on over 30 topics right to your desktop–any time, just in time, and just in case you need it. Each topic includes:

1. Core Concepts: essential information in an easy-to-read format

2. Practical tips, tools, checklists, and planning worksheets

3. Interactive practice exercises and audio examples to enhance your learning

Try out two complimentary topics for Harvard ManageMentor® PLUS
by going to: **http://eLearning.harvardbusinessonline.org**

Harvard ManageMentor is available as a full online program with over 30 topics for $195 or as individual downloadable topics for $19.95 each. Selected topics are also available as printed Harvard ManageMentor Business Guides for $12.95 each and on CD-ROM (4 topics each) for only $49.95. For site license and volume discount pricing Call 800.795.5200 (outside the U.S. and Canada: 617.783.7888) or visit http://eLearning.harvardbusinessonline.org.

HARVARD
ManageMentor®

An online resource for
managers in a hurry